Atheneum Books by John Christopher Fine

Sunken Ships and Treasure
Oceans in Peril

Oceans in Peril

OCEANS IN PERIL

by John Christopher Fine

illustrated with photographs

by the author

FOREWORD BY

PRINCE ALBERT OF MONACO

Atheneum　　·　　*New York*

Atheneum
Macmillan Publishing Company
866 Third Avenue, New York, NY 10022
Collier Macmillan Canada, Inc.

Type set by Arcata Graphics/Kingsport, Kingsport, Tennessee
Printed and bound by Fairfield Graphics, Fairfield, Pennsylvania
Designed by Mary Ahern
First Edition

10   9   8   7   6   5   4   3   2

Library of Congress Cataloging-in-Publication Data

Fine, John Christopher.   Oceans in peril.

Bibliography: p. 134
Includes index.
SUMMARY: Examines plant and animal resources found in
the sea, the effects of human intrusion and pollution, and
possible solutions to the threat posed to our oceans.
1. Marine pollution—Juvenile literature.   2. Marine
biology—Juvenile literature.   3. Marine resources—
Juvenile literature.   [1. Marine resources conservation.
3. Marine pollution.   3. Marine ecology]   I. Title.
GC1085.F56   1987   363.7'394   86-26546
ISBN 0-689-31328-4

CONTENTS

FOREWORD

I was very touched by the kind thought of John Fine, who asked me to preface his book, OCEANS IN PERIL. The Princes of Monaco have always had great interest in, and passion for, the sea.

From antiquity, the people of Monaco, living on a modest circle of land facing the Mediterranean—surrounded by the Alps—view the sea, which not only provides nourishment, but presents a challenge for adventure; a route for civilization and commerce.

The Lords, then the Princes of Monaco, sometimes warriors, sometimes scholars, raised this passion for the sea to the highest level, to understand and defend it.

Prince Albert the First, one of the founders of oceanography, revealed the immense riches and inexhaustible resources of the oceans. He dedicated himself to scientific research, especially from great ocean depths. Beginning in 1910, Albert the First exhibited his collection of specimens from the world's oceans in the now famous Oceanographic Museum in Monte Carlo.

Concerned about the protection of the oceans, Albert the First spoke out against overfishing, taking steps to maintain intact the wilderness and richness of nature.

Facing an immense task, my father, Prince Rainier, guided by the same aspirations, concentrated his efforts on the protection of the sea that bathes the shores of the Principality of Monaco.

For thirty years, Prince Rainier has presided over the International Commission for Scientific Exploration of the

Author John Christopher Fine receives a medal from S.A.S. Prince Albert of Monaco during the World Film Festival at Juan-les-Pins. The hereditary ruler of Monaco (son of Princess Grace and Prince Rainier), Prince Albert is a direct descendant of Albert I of Monaco, a pioneer ocean explorer, considered the father of modern oceanography, and founder of Monaco's famed Oceanographic Museum. Fine, in turn, presented Prince Albert with a specially engraved knife made of materials recovered during the Statue of Liberty restoration, along with a message of friendship and good will from the President of the United States.

Mediterranean, an organization of seventeen countries, coordinating research in the context of protection of the sea.

In 1960, my father denounced a plan to dump 6000 barrels of radioactive waste into the Mediterranean.

Particularly attentive to the Barcelona Convention and

resolutions of international organizations, Prince Rainier initiated a tripartite commission composed of France, Italy and Monaco. This commission created a pilot zone for surveillance of the sea between Hyères and Genoa and implemented joint actions for environmental protection of the sea. The RAMOGE accords, as the project is called, regularly pursues this work; unfortunately too slowly.

Concerned about practical ways of protecting the sea, Prince Rainier recently declared, "Everything has been said about the dangers of pollution, of the risks that threaten human life, about the grave threats to plant and animal marine life, particularly in the Mediterranean, but what have we really done for the protection of all this natural wealth?"

In order to set an example—even on the reduced scale of our country—in 1976, my father created a law setting aside an underwater preserve near the shores of Monaco. In this preserve, motor boating and spearfishing are prohibited, creating a zone where animal and plant life, notably the posidonia, are protected.

We hope this short overview, describing some of the actions of the Princes of Monaco that coincide with the object of this book, will raise the reader's consciousness about the importance of the problem and make the reader our associate in the protection of nature and the ocean wilderness.

Convinced of the importance of this task, I wish that the splendid underwater scenes, pictures which we can still admire at Ocean Festivals around the world, remain beautiful proof that humankind will have succeeded in mastering the means and methods at our disposal so as not to destroy our natural heritage. We must remember the old adage, that "Science without conscience will ruin the world."

ALBERT OF MONACO
Hereditary Prince, Marquis des Baux

Oceans in Peril

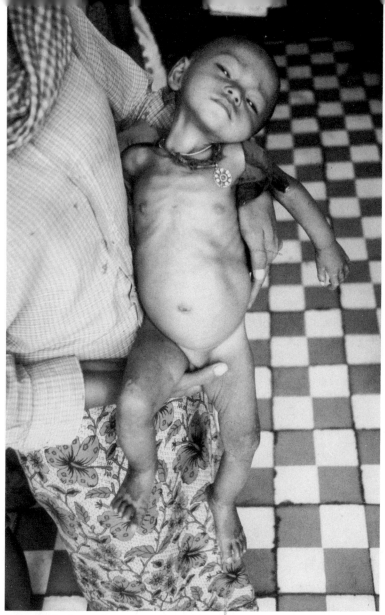

*We depend on the oceans for food. Now and in the future.
Famine is a horrible thing to witness. Starvation and
malnutrition are a reality in a world with ever-growing
populations and less land available for cultivation. Protection
of the oceans now will insure their availability as a source of
food for future generations.*

INTRODUCTION

I have always been drawn to the oceans; I took up diving when I was about six years old, and the sea has provided a source of inspiration for my writing. When I don my scuba equipment and dive beneath the surface, I see that life in the ocean realm has a special fascination and beauty that we are only beginning to understand. What I have always understood—what was always clear from my exploration of the underwater world—was that the oceans are a vast reservoir of life, a source of food and nourishment for most of the world. The oceans hold the key to solving the crisis of hunger today, as well as to establishing a future source of food for the world.

Think about it. In forty years the population on the Earth will be about double what it is today, according to economists' predictions. Yet today, in this world of modern technology, twenty-four people die from hunger every minute; eighteen of them are children under five years of age. Each day and every day of the year, 35,000 people starve to death.

How will an increasing world population be fed once the space available for cultivation is taken for human habitation, when the soil is depleted of nutrients by overplanting, when fertilizers made from petroleum products and harmful insecticides made from chemicals become impossible to use? The answers are immediately apparent—we will look to the oceans for food.

While the directive—go fish and farm the sea—is an immediate response to the present crisis of world hunger and the future demands for food, it is also apparent that humans are seriously polluting the seas and oceans, often using these important water resources as an all-purpose dump.

ممنوع الصيد بالحربة
واخذ المرجان

SPEERFISHING
CORALS PICKING
NOT ALLOWED

While a teacher might take points off for spelling, the message on this sign, posted by Red Sea divers in the Sinai—in Arabic and English—gets an "A" for effort. Preservation of this delicate marine reserve will mean economic benefit for those who earn their living taking visitors diving.

We've all seen signs at the waterfront that say "No Bathing Allowed," or "It Is Illegal to Take Shellfish from These Waters." News broadcasts warn about bans on eating certain fish because of the high levels of toxic elements in their flesh, which are a health risk to humans. These warnings are only the first indications of a crisis that is getting worse. The oceans are in peril.

With careful husbandry—strict safeguards and conservation measures that will protect the oceans from pollution—the harm can be controlled. The responsibility for ocean conservation is everyone's responsibility.

We generally take care of things that belong to us, knowing that if we're careless or reckless or misuse something, it won't last. Well, we should have that same sense of personal responsibility toward the oceans and the creatures that live there.

While we consider some of the problems and perils of the oceans, we will also look to possible solutions that will help the oceans survive. The fate of the oceans is directly tied to human survival, an important relationship to understand and one we will explore in this book.

When I lecture and show slides and films describing problems facing the oceans, the most frequently asked question is: What can I do? People asking that question most often want a short, simple answer that can be immediately translated into action. They want an immediate way to resolve complex problems of pollution and abuse. Why don't they stop the dumping? Why don't government officials make them stop it? These are some of the angry questions I get.

While there are few quick, sure-fire answers to the problems, there *is* one thing we can all do. We can make a personal commitment, a personal pledge, an individual appeal for bal-

Our seashores and waterways are littered with waste. Here on the shore of New York City's East River a homeless person has built a temporary shelter amid the litter and debris that chokes the banks of the waterway.

anced use of the oceans and ocean conservation. That's the first step: concern and a willingness to care.

As a trustee of the International Oceanographic Foundation, I drafted and proposed a charter for the oceans—a pledge. It has no force and effect in law, but then, sometimes human conscience is more powerful than any library of laws; human sentiment can be stronger than an army.

In endorsing this Ocean Charter, the President of the United States, Ronald Reagan, said: "I am pleased to commend the officers and trustees of the International Oceanographic Foundation for their commitment to balanced use of the seas and responsible attitudes toward ocean conservation as expressed in your 'Ocean Charter.'

"It is vital that the imagination and vision with which our nation addresses the economic potential of the ocean be equaled by our concern for the protection of the marine biosystem. The Foundation is making a valuable contribution to the ongoing effort to protect the health of the vast and irreplaceable treasure which covers three quarters of our planet."

To answer the question—what can I do?—simply and quickly: Learn all you can about the way the oceans support life, how the ocean systems function, the way creatures interact to form a natural ecosystem. Join and become active in organizations like the International Oceanographic Foundation, whose publications, projects, museum, and activities will keep you informed and involved in ocean issues. Care. Care about the quality of life around you, the quality of life of other human beings who may be less fortunate. Care about the other living creatures who share this planet with us.

Once you've learned enough to understand the importance of the oceans in our lives now and in the future, make an individual pledge. Commit yourself to the principles of The Ocean Charter, which is the first step in becoming a responsible citizen of the sea.

Author John Christopher Fine (short sleeves) with the pioneer of modern diving, Philippe Tailliez, at Port Cros, France. Here in an area of a protected reserve, the men witness pollution in all its forms, plastic discards, human waste, litter, and non-degradable debris.

THE OCEAN CHARTER

The oceans belong to no one; they belong to all of us, so they belong to me. It is my ocean, my sea, my water. I am a warden of this wilderness. All the creatures that dwell there are part of my responsibility, everyone's responsibility.

We who live on land have everything to do with the sea even if we have nothing to do with it directly. By being responsible for the oceans we are responsible for the quality of our lives and the quality of life of other living things for now and in the future.

The ocean is important to all of us. We must treat the ocean as something precious that belongs to us. Though we cannot own it nor possess it, it is ours to protect and preserve, to use wisely and with care, to enjoy and explore. We must claim the ocean for the good of all living creatures.

I proclaim, as each of us must proclaim: These are my waters. I pledge myself as a warden of the wilderness, a guardian of nature; vanguard of the ocean realm and sentinel of the seas.

It is my ocean.

In Hong Kong, amid the crowded anchorage of Aberdeen, thousands of people depend on the food they are able to catch each day in the harbor. In most parts of the world people depend on the water resources for their daily meals.

1

Food from the Sea

"I'M HUNGRY." How often have we said those words? How often have we said, "I'm hungry," without really being hungry, having only the desire to eat for the pleasurable satisfaction of eating, rather than eating to satisfy the physical need for food? The average person who reads these lines need only move a short distance to a cupboard or refrigerator to satisfy any desire for food, to pick up a telephone and "send out" for food, or leave a comfortable dwelling and travel a short distance to a market or grocery store, restaurant, sweet shop, or fast-food emporium to tank up on food or drink, satisfying any desire.

In contrast, for the average person in the world at large, being hungry is a daily reality that is satisfied by subsistence—farming or fishing each day for the food that will be eaten that evening.

The reality is that there are one billion chronically undernourished people in the world today. Each year, thirteen to eighteen million people die from hunger. That means thirty-five thousand people die from the effects of starvation each day. Every minute twenty-four people starve to death; eighteen of those victims are children.

There are almost five billion people in the world today, three billion more than the total world population in 1930. The world has not increased in size since 1800, when only one billion people inhabited this planet. No more space was added to the earth between 1982 and 1983, when ninety-two million more people were added to the world population. To feed all these people, and economists say that by the year 2025 there will be more than eight billion people on earth, more food must be harvested.

The land is tired. We have pushed our land resources to the limit of their productivity. Nutrients in the soil have been depleted year after year by planting crops. Farmers supplement the feeble nutrients in the soil with fertilizers derived from petroleum products, fossil fuels which in their development and use degrade the overall environment.

We increase the food from the soil by using pesticides, insecticides, and herbicides to kill unwanted vermin, insects, and weeds that compete for the crops. But the chemicals that eliminate pests and weeds also kill and destroy the environment. We eliminate the wilderness by population expansion, building, and planting, thus diminishing the ability of nature to cope with future demands for fertile land, diminishing as well the reservoir, the savings bank of life on terrestrial earth.

Most of the world already depends on the oceans for food. For these people, food does not mean sending out for a midnight snack of pizza or ice cream; food means the difference between life and death.

A moment's thought and all of us will conclude that the seas and oceans of the world are the fountainhead of life, the source for our present and future needs, the space where we will turn to cultivate the food needed to feed the rapidly growing population on earth.

Whether the oceans will be able to continue to provide the growing world population with food is both a question that remains unanswered and an issue that remains unresolved. Perhaps the best way to understand the importance of food from the sea is to listen to experts, people who go to sea each day to catch fish, who observe firsthand the problems and perils of the oceans.

"Now you trawl six hours and you bring back this many fish," said Ed Maluzewski, a veteran commercial fisherman from Avon, New Jersey, cupping his two hands together to show how few fish were caught. "I just have a day boat. I can't go out and stay out overnight, fishing sixty miles offshore where there are still some fish. Along the coast it's finished," Ed said sternly, describing the sad state of Atlantic offshore fishing.

"With all this pollution, dumping of everything from toxic wastes to sewage, there's nothing left," Charlie Stratton added. Charlie, a veteran diver and long-time observer of the Atlantic Ocean, has known Ed a long time. The two men reminisced about what it was like to fish and explore the offshore reaches of the Atlantic before years of continual pollution all but eradicated the fishing, clamming, and scalloping grounds.

"They tell me sulfiding is not the right word to use," Charlie said, looking at his friend. "But when I dive down to the bottom and reach into the sea with my hands and scoop it up, it's a black material that's there. When you bring up a sample it smells like rotten eggs, just like sulfide. I don't know. . . ." Charlie paused.

"You used to go out and come back with a deck full of fish," Ed put in. "Not now. It's all changed. I could tell you stories . . ." the commercial fisherman started to say, then just shook his head, dismayed by the condition of the ocean environment that has been the source of his livelihood for many, many years.

"I'm going to a meeting tomorrow," Charlie said. "This

Veteran skipper Charlie Stratton scans the horizon looking for evidence of illegal dumping of toxic-wastes in the Atlantic.

group is holding hearings on the state of the ocean off New Jersey. I've written this out and I'm going to tell them that it's getting worse. I go to a lot of meetings. It doesn't do any good. I just tell them to look at the price of fish in the market," Charlie added, making a point about the problem in a way everyone could understand. The scarcer the fish, the higher the price at market.

What Charlie and Ed were saying about the Atlantic, fishermen all over the world have been witnessing as well. Overfishing and pollution have reduced alarmingly the stocks of commercial food fish worldwide. More boats go out, run farther offshore, and stay out longer, only to catch fewer fish than ever before.

Some nations operate major high-seas fisheries with factory ships, which operate in much the same way that organized whaling interests did years ago, when they nearly wiped out the population of whales. Everything is brought up in the trawls. The ocean bottom is scraped clean of life. Inedible species are ground up for animal feed or fertilizer. This form of fishing will clearly destroy the world's ocean resources by depleting all breeding stocks and destroying the food upon which the edible fish live.

FREDERIC Dumas, a renowned spearfisherman in the thirties, before the invention of scuba equipment, inspired Philippe Tailliez with his prowess. Dumas still lives on the Mediterranean, at Port Issol Beach, north of Toulon. Tailliez and Dumas dived together, spearing great merous, Mediterranean groupers that inhabited the underwater reaches of the beautiful, rocky coastline. Eventually, Tailliez brought a third man into their special union, and they came to be known as the Three Musketeers of the Sea. The third man was Jacques-Yves Cousteau.

Spearfishing remains a popular sport. In some places people hunt fish with spears as a means of obtaining food from the sea. But spearfishing for sport is practiced with sophisticated guns that leave nothing to chance, especially when divers wear scuba tanks, giving them autonomy underwater to stalk their quarry. There are international spearfishing championships organized by the World Underwater Federation, but spearfishing is nothing in popularity when compared to line fishing and deep-sea sport fishing.

Whether spearfishing and sport fishing are still valid pursuits when the fish taken are not to be consumed out of need is a subject debated emotionally around the world. At a recent general assembly of the World Underwater Federation, a motion was put on the floor that would have ended spearfishing as an internationally sanctioned sport. The motion was defeated, but the topic remains an emotional one, especially among divers like Jacques-Yves Cousteau, who has said no in absolute terms to spearfishing in view of the need to respect and conserve the marine environment.

Perhaps the best reflection on the issue was made by Frederic Dumas. This dean of free-diving and undersea hunting, a man who has observed the undersea environment for half a century, whose experience and knowledge date from the beginning of human penetration of the sea in modern times, observed, "There's a confidence, an enormous curiosity, fish for man in the underwater environment. Animals on land fear man." Frederic Dumas was speaking from the enormous terraced tree-house he built in his backyard at Port Issol, so he could look out at the sea.

"Spearfishing is a good sport, but it kills fish. It destroys the fish and they don't come back. I made a little calculation. A spearfisherman who started diving when he was seventeen years old, now he's fifty-two and still hunts with his spear gun. I know such a person, he's been spearfishing for thirty-five years. This spearfisherman says he's seen nothing changed in the underwater environment. He can say that. Except, me, I started spearfishing long before this spearfisherman. I began on the beach in front of my house." Dumas motioned with his hand to the vast expanse of blue beyond the beach.

"Each day I hunted fish, I had to swim three hundred meters farther to find fish. These spearfishermen started hunt-

Author John Christopher Fine (left), Philippe Tailliez (middle), and Frederic Dumas (glasses) discuss Dumas's early recollections about the state of the Mediterranean environment.

ing when there was nothing left. They started after we had destroyed everything, me and my friends," Dumas said emphatically, this elder statesman of the sea describing the effects of many years of spearfishing on the marine environment.

"They have a brain, fish, and they use it. The Mediterranean coast is very rocky, and the territory of fish, the territory they inhabit, is very narrow, like a river is wide. We kill the largest fish, the fish which reproduce. Those fish that remain in this territory are afraid of divers and descend into the depths and we don't see them. It is impossible to explain this fact to the public; they never knew the sea before," Frederic Dumas said.

What Frederic Dumas said in simple, straightforward terms is what scientific studies have been pointing out for years. Anyone on shore watching fishermen come into port on the Mediterranean coast, observing their poor catch, will know what Dumas says is true. It is rare that divers on the Mediterranean coast today, especially along the populated and crowded areas of the French and Italian Riviera, see any fish to speak of, save for small, inedible species.

As difficult as it is for Frederic Dumas to explain to those who never knew the sea as he knew it, a pioneer visitor to the underwater wilderness, it is even more difficult to convince people that everything in nature has a place, and that wanton, purposeless killing and waste cannot be tolerated. Spearfishing is no different from sea angling. Many anglers catch great marlin and sailfish, not for food but for the thrill of it, leaving the fish behind them to rot or using the fish only as a trophy, wasting the food.

On the beautiful island of Tahiti, on a small reef in the lagoon where I taught students to dive and see the wonders of tropical life, a small scorpion fish lived near the rocks. The scorpion fish has poisonous dorsal spines, which it uses for defense. A visitor, diving for the first time, surfaced excitedly. He climbed up on the dock and asked me if he could borrow my knife. I found out that the visitor wanted to kill the little scorpion fish, and refused to lend the knife. I tried to explain that the little fish, if observed and left alone, was harmless. It was an excellent subject for teaching divers about underwater life. I pointed out that the little scorpion fish could always be found near the rocks where it lived.

Unconvinced, the visitor disappeared, and I went back to my classes. When I surfaced later, the visitor was on the dock, a small group of people gathered around him. The little scorpion fish was impaled on a screwdriver. At first I was angry, then just frustrated, by this unthinking, uneducated, and unnecessary act.

The act is nothing standing alone. Yet like all such acts, it is a symbol of human arrogance and human intrusion on nature—intrusion without the comprehension that if we are to count on the oceans for food, we must respect them and take what we need without greed or waste.

2

The Magic Island Where Life Depends on the Sea

THERE is a place on the island where piles of conch shells rise up like mountains on the seashore. The dead shells are bleached white by the sun, all with a nick out of the end where fishermen broke into the shell, inserted a knife, and forced the living mollusk out of its home. The conch is food, cooked up as fritters, eaten raw in conch salad, or pounded and sliced to be made tender then fried in a pan. But the conch has almost completely disappeared in the shallow waters around this island, where once there was a plentiful supply.

People who live on an island depend on the sea for food. Isolated, cut off from the rest of the world except for occasional supply boats and airplanes that bring mail, hardware, and visitors, an island, in order for its economy and people to thrive, must have food from the sea readily available and fairly easy to come by. On Bonaire, where most of the conch have been fished out in shallow water, marine biologist Robie Hensen is at work on a restoration project that is attempting to replenish conch populations, in the hope of assuring the island of a future supply of food.

"Conch is a shallow-water animal," Robie said, "but it's fished out of the shallow water. You do find them where there are algae to feed on—I've seen conch as deep as one hundred and twenty meters. Here on Bonaire you find them in deep water, about forty meters. That's where I go to collect the eggs for the restoration project."

The depletion of conch around the shallow waters of Bonaire, a twenty-four-mile-long island located about fifty miles off the coast of Venezuela in the Western Caribbean, is similar to the depletion of marine food supplies worldwide. Had there been careful management and common-sense guidelines imposed at an early stage, then the people would

On the island of Bonaire in the Dutch Antilles, a conch fisherman stares out at the bay. In the background are piles of conch shells, silent testimony to the overfishing that has depleted the mollusk, an important source of food for the island.

have been assured of a limitless supply of food. Greed, which fostered fishing at a rate faster than the animal's ability to reproduce, nearly wiped out the entire population. Now the few mollusks that can be found around Bonaire are usually in deep water, beyond the reach of the conch fishermen. Robie Hensen is concerned about the future of his island.

"The conch is fished out. Not only by islanders but by people from Venezuela and Curaçao," Robie explained, pointing off in the direction of Curaçao, the more populated adjoining island, about thirty miles east of Bonaire. "You see those fruit boats in the harbor? They come to Bonaire from Venezuela with fruit. They used to sell their cargo of fruit then go to the other side of the island, fill up with conch, then go back to Venezuela. They have very large holds, so they took a lot of conch on each trip," Robie said, describing one of the ways in which the conch were depleted around the island.

Robie, the son of a Dutch father and Antillean mother, was born on Curaçao, where he developed an interest in animals. "When you live on an island," Robie said with a smile, "marine biology is the way to go." He did his undergraduate training at McGill University in Canada and graduate work at the University of Miami. For Robie, an offer from the governments of Aruba, Curaçao, and Bonaire—islands in the Dutch Antilles with a great deal of autonomy from Holland—to construct a marine lab and undertake a major conch-raising and restoration project presented a wonderful challenge.

"The lab was built by the end of 1981, and while it was going up I did a lot of research around the islands to find populations of conch that were mating. In March 1982, we started with the conch egg masses, and by May of that year we had our first juvenile conch," Robie said.

The conch lays an egg mass that may contain as many as two hundred thousand eggs in long strands resembling large shredded wheat biscuits. Once the eggs were collected, workers at the conch-restoration project examined them under a microscope to make sure they were fertile. The outside of the egg masses were then sterilized, to protect the fertile eggs from contamination by bacteria that could destroy them. Conch eggs hatch in five days into thin-shelled larvae with winglike structures called velums. These larvae are called veligers, or veliger larvae. "We keep the veliger larvae in suspension in these large tanks," Robie explained, "feeding them one-celled algae, which we grow here." He pointed to large glass bottles containing green algae.

The tanks in the lab were filled with sterilized and filtered sea water. "These larvae are no bigger than a pinprick," Robie said. "They remain as larvae for about a month. By that time the two wings have grown into three pairs of wings, and the larvae have grown to eight-tenths of a millimeter. The shell itself is about four-tenths of a millimeter. At that stage the animal is able to metamorphose, to change from one stage of development to the next. We induce this change, or metamorphosis, by adding an extract from red algae we prepare ourselves. Other animals, such as the abalone, have similar life cycles," Robie explained.

"The reason this system evolved in nature," he continued, "was to give the larvae, which have very little chance to survive in the ocean, a chance to settle and metamorphose in shallow water where algae grow. Larvae can remain as larvae for up to six months at sea. But if they come in contact with algae, they metamorphose and sink to the bottom. Here you see a picture of the metamorphosis." Robie pointed to a chart on the laboratory wall. "The conch now have small black shells. We leave them in these tanks for about a week until the shells get harder, feeding them algae. Then we put them in the outside tanks for three to five months. When they are about one inch in size, we release them." Robie added.

Author John Christopher Fine with conch being raised on Bonaire. Work in raising and releasing conch is defeated if conservation rules are not enforced.

Release of the baby conch has been done in both shallow and deeper water. The project thus far has released about two million conch to the ocean water surrounding the islands.

The juvenile conch continue to grow around and around, forming the shell from the top, or pointed, end. When conch become adults, which takes two and a half to three years, their shells develop a flaring lip. Once the flaring lip develops, the conch do not grow any larger, but their shells become thicker with age.

"This one is two and a half years old and this one is thirty years old," Robie said, holding up two conch shells. "They can live about thirty to forty years. Radioactive isotopes have dated one conch shell on Bermuda Island to about thirty-five years old," Robie explained. But the population of conch has and is being depleted before they even have time to breed.

"On these islands—Bonaire, Aruba, and Curaçao—there is a ban on taking any conch. It is forbidden to take conch for a couple of years, and the ban is still on.

"But the ban is not enforced," the youthful biologist said sadly. "Nothing is done about it. The project of raising the juvenile conch is successful. The young conch released from the lab have a survival rate of from sixty to seventy percent. But once they grow to eating size, the fishermen are very efficient in taking all the conch they can find, so survival after they become one year old is zero. Conch should not be taken until the flaring lip develops, but a size limit is not enforced either. It is politics on these islands. The fishermen are a large voting block. I'm not a policeman. They pay me to grow conch and put them in the sea and keep my mouth shut. But it doesn't make sense," the young biologist declared, describing why the conch-restoration project wasn't working.

The economics of the problem has already taken a toll on the small island, where there are too few conch to take for food. "We import a lot of conch meat. If we allow this project to work and there is conservation, we will not have to spend our money outside the island and we will provide fishermen with employment. Now the conch meat comes in from Venezuela, Belize, and the Dominican Republic," Robie explained.

In nature, survival of the conch larvae and juvenile shells is haphazard at best. Of the two-hundred-thousand-plus eggs in a cluster laid by a breeding conch, many fall prey to the fish and animals in the sea that are plankton feeders, that eat small animals floating in the water. All kinds of marine worms and small fish devour larvae. Juvenile conch are the food of hermit crabs and octopus, and as conch grow, they become the favorite food of rays, turtles, and the worst enemy of all, humans.

While both ecology and economy are directly and indirectly linked all over the world, nowhere is this more apparent than on an island. The marine lab on Bonaire is at work on many other projects affecting that island's environment and economy. The lab is experimenting with projects to raise tropical fish and food fish, as well as to protect endangered species.

"We're looking into raising aquarium fish, reef and tropical fish, for the simple reason that there's a huge market of collectors in the United States and elsewhere. We'll be doing something for the protection of the reefs, because it will prevent people from taking fish from the wild. In taking the fish large parts of the reefs are destroyed," Robie Hensen said, explaining yet another aspect of his work on Bonaire.

Protection of Bonaire's reefs is another vital key to the island's economy and thus its survival. Even the license plates on Bonaire's vehicles proclaim it as "The Diver's Paradise." With the increasing popularity of sport scuba diving and snorkling, the clear, clean water and magnificent shallow reefs around Bonaire have created a major tourist industry, with thousands of divers visiting the island each year to explore the coral reefs.

Responding to the challenge of preserving the natural beauty of Bonaire's undersea environment, American expatriate Captain Don Stewart began a campaign years ago to make the entire island a marine park and sanctuary, where the taking of coral and shells and spearfishing would be prohibited.

Captain Don succeeded in part of his mission when he obtained the cooperation of island authorities and dive operators to create permanent moorings for boats. That way boats taking divers out to the reefs would not have to drop their anchors on them, which can destroy the coral growth below.

Captain Don Stewart with kids on the island of Bonaire, teaching them about the importance of conservation. Captain Don was the subject of a Dondi *cartoon strip emphasizing the importance of conserving natural resources. The kids, who have pledged themselves as Friends of the Sea, were given Underwater Society of America pins while listening to Don's important message about ocean conservation.*

Anchor damage once or twice is not fatal to the reef environment as a whole. But repeated anchoring over the dive sites destroys them in a short time, destroying as well the reason visitors come to Bonaire.

With permanent moorings and conservation rules in force, Captain Don has embarked on another phase of his mission. He has undertaken something that, he says, "will come to occupy the balance of my life." Part of that mission is to educate people about ocean conservation.

Captain Don, who arrived at Bonaire in his sailing ship twenty-five years ago and stayed on to explore the reefs and teach diving, was the subject of a comic strip series by Irwin Hasen, the cartoonist who created the famous Dondi. In the strip, Dondi visits the island of "Bonairy" and is taught to dive by "Cap'n Don."

"At that time I wanted to explain the ocean to our youth. I'm a bit of a showman, so when Irwin Hasen proposed a comic strip, I went for it," Captain Don said, digging out the costume he wore for the cartoons.

"I talked about preservation, conservation, just plain common sense," Don explained. "I've been interviewed eight hundred times. I've stressed, over those eight hundred interviews, conservation.

"The end result is, you do all kinds of crazy things to attract attention. It's a small island, and when writers come here, they look for a character. That's me. What they've done with these articles sometimes makes me grind my teeth," Don said, saddened by the fact that so few writers have helped him carry his message of marine resource conservation to the world.

In spite of Captain Don's impatience that his message is taking too long to be heard and still longer to be listened to, many young people are learning responsibility toward ocean resources. In Irwin Hasen's comic strip, Dondi tells the world: "There's one thing I learned here in Bonairy that I can tell my pals back home. I learned that it's just as important to protect the underwater environment and keep it clean as it is to protect the air and land above water."

What Dondi learned from "Cap'n Don," his creator, cartoonist Irwin Hasen learned from Captain Don himself. "He taught me how to snorkle. Finally Don took me out on a boat. For me that was really something," Irwin Hasen admitted. "I'm not a great swimmer. But Don pushed me off the boat. We'd been training in three to four feet of water in front of Habitat, Don's diving lodge on Bonaire. Now the boat was anchored over deep water on the reef," Irwin said. He added with a smile, "It was one of the greatest experiences of my life. I'll never forget it, watching another world," he said, describing his first experience snorkling over Bonaire's reefs.

Cartoonist Irwin Hasen sketching out the famous caricature of Dondi *with a message to people everywhere to protect the* oceans.

Dondi's *message*.

"The reefs are an essential part of this planet. We must not corrupt the oceans as we've corrupted the world above," Irwin Hasen warned, sketching out a message by Dondi to young people everywhere to save the seas.

A FORMER New Yorker who moved to Bonaire twelve years ago, Morey Ruza, who works with Captain Don at Habitat, is quick to point up the importance of reef management on

Bonaire. "We realize that the most fragile part of our environment here is the reef. We've decided that we're going to cut some of the buoys and moorings. We are going to close off some of the popular diving spots. We'll give them a couple of years' rest. Reef management is important. By closing off some of the spots, the coral, which invariably gets broken by too many careless divers, will have a chance to come back," Morey explained.

"Natural problems affect our reefs as well. The coral had a blight a few years back. After the blight, only the tips of the coral came back. Then two years ago a storm passed through. The storm and waves knocked over all of the staghorn and elkhorn coral. Where before only the tips were growing, now there is new growth and the coral is coming back again," Morey said.

Even industry on Bonaire depends on the sea. On the flats at the southern tip of Bonaire, a solar salt works takes advantage of the year-round sunshine on the island to evaporate sea water and make salt. The flats are flooded, and then the brine is condensed as the fresh water is evaporated away by the sun's rays. Six to eight inches (fifteen to twenty centimeters) of salt remains in the flats every year. The salt is scraped up by machines, washed, stored in great piles, and exported by ship. In olden days, slaves were employed to mine the salt. The huts they used still remain near the salt works.

Fresh water for the island is made from sea water in Bonaire's desalination plant. If ever the oceans surrounding Bonaire became contaminated with chemical, bacteriological, or other wastes, drinking water would have to be brought in by boat at great expense.

Fishermen on Bonaire are permitted to capture sea turtles, although the taking of their eggs from nesting beaches is prohibited. Fish are mostly caught by line and sold that day in the markets on the island. There are many species of lizards on Bonaire, and some, like the iguana, are especially prized by islanders for use in making soup.

Bonaire has a rich history of Indian habitation that dates to long before the island's discovery in 1499 by one of Christopher Columbus's captains, Alonzo de Ojeda. The navigator on that voyage was Amerigo Matteo Vespucci, for whom America is named. Passing through a succession of colonial powers, Bonaire was finally colonized by the Dutch in 1636. The island is an autonomous part of the Kingdom of the Netherlands. It is governed by a lieutenant governor appointed by the Queen of Holland's governor on Curaçao, and is represented in the islands' legislative body, called the Staten, or Parliament. Bonaire also has its own Island Council.

Tourism makes up an important part of Bonaire's economy. People on the island are aware that they must not kill the goose that lays their golden eggs. If the quality of life on Bonaire's reefs is destroyed, then the tourists will not return. Although Bonaire started down the same path that resulted in the destruction of the beauty and natural balance on other islands in the Caribbean, this island is aware that uncontrolled construction of hotels, condominiums, and dwellings will bring more people than the island's resources can handle. Overpopulation by tourists will not only ruin Bonaire's sense of adventure and discovery—it will also strain the ability of the natural systems to cope with the pressures of additional people and waste.

"On the whole there are only 350 to 400 rooms on the island, and that includes bungalows," said Dick Breukink, the assistant manager of the Bonaire Beach Hotel, the largest hotel on the island.

"We want to keep it on the low scale so it does not become like a bus stop," Dick added, going on to explain how the hotel has instituted a system of reusing waste water to water plants around the grounds; a filtration system and

pipes drip water to the garden so it does not have to be watered. Conservation measures include the use of special coded keys that are attached to guests' hotel room keys. The coded keys must be inserted in the room air conditioners to make them work. Thus the air conditioners are used only when people are in the rooms, saving energy and preventing waste.

The same responsible attitude could be observed when the hotel decided to remove an old stone jetty to give beach-goers more room. The stones had been in the water a long time and served as a habitat for attracting marine organisms. As soon as the owners of the hotel's scuba concession Al Catalfumo and Eddy Statia, saw workmen begin to dismantle the jetty, they hurried over in a rowboat and began moving the stones into deeper water, where the reef could continue to grow and provide shallow-water viewing for inexperienced snorklers swimming from the hotel beach.

While most people assume that kids living on an island know how to swim, that's not always true. Even though islanders earn their livelihood from the sea and are never out of sight of the ocean on any day in their lives, many never learn to swim. On Bonaire, Captain Don calls his island-born divemasters "cowboys," saying that if they weren't a special breed of adventurous young people, he could never get them to learn to dive and become underwater guides.

Learning is the key to being able to appreciate the marine environment. Young people learning to swim and dive on Bonaire, overcoming their fear of the water and things they

Captain Don Stewart diving over the memorial flag he and Percy Sweetnan planted in the waters off Bonaire, commemorating those who have devoted their lives to ocean conservation, who dive no more.

don't fully understand, will become better citizens of the sea, truly at home on their island.

"Kids here who never snorkle or dive don't realize what they have to lose if the environment on Bonaire is destroyed," Robie Hensen said, adding, "many are caught up in the American television culture. They want things they see on television programs. They don't see how in big cities, and even in small cities, industry and carelessness have polluted the environment. They don't appreciate what real beauty they have here at home."

Bonaire is, as Cap'n Don told Dondi in the comic strip, "a mountain in the sea," whose undersea mountains and reefs are the island's life blood. The waters surrounding Bonaire provide food for its inhabitants and a bounty of discovery for visitors.

For former Californian Captain Don, the reefs and marine life are not just the means by which he earns his living. The wonder of the undersea provides the inspiration for his life.

"This is the thing," Don said, interrupting himself to make a sweeping gesture out toward the reefs, where an orange sunset was shimmering off the water. "Get people to pay attention now. Look what is happening to all those baby conch that are being put back. People have got to listen. Conservation is only common sense. . . ." His voice trailed off. He was hoping that taking kids on his lap, reading them the Dondi comic strip and telling them the story of the conch, would make them responsible citizens of the sea, deputized to carry his message to young people everywhere.

One of the permanent moorings Captain Don and others like Eddy Statia and Al Catalfumo have installed around the island of Bonaire so that boats do not have to use anchors, which destroy coral.

There are important lessons about conservation and the results of failing to conserve ocean resources to be learned from Bonaire. The island is a "proud country risen from the sea," as sung in Bonaire's patriotic hymn. All of us must join Captain Don in a commitment to ". . . preservation, conservation, just plain common sense," to protect and preserve our ocean wilderness on Bonaire and everywhere.

3

The Coral Reef

U NDERWATER mountains
of stone," Charles Darwin called them, describing the coral
atolls and reefs he observed during a voyage aboard his
research vessel, *Beagle,* in 1836. They are mountains, greater
than any mountains on land, living mountains, built layer
upon layer in the undersea over many millions of years. For
coral is an animal. Regardless of its forms, coral begins life
as free-swimming larvae.

There are two ways in which coral reproduces. The first
is through the release into the water of sperm which fertilize
eggs inside other coral polyps, resulting in the production
of larvae. Larvae eventually leave the polyp and drift in the
water, kept afloat by microscopic, hairlike wands. When the
larvae settle on a substrate, they anchor. Once the coral polyp
is anchored, it develops by a second means, known as asexual
budding. A polyp grows and splits off from the first, developing into a distinct and separate adult structure. In the enormity
of coral reefs, which in some cases consist of barrier reefs
hundreds of miles long, there are many different species and
forms of coral. The growth of the reef takes place over many
millions of years.

Beautiful coral polyps, their delicate tentacles extended for feeding, are mighty builders in the sea. To exist, they must have a clean and clear environment where sunlight can penetrate, free from silt and harmful waste.

Coral reefs flourish and grow only where the water is clear enough for sunlight to penetrate and where the water temperature is warm.

The polyps feed on small, microscopic animal organisms in the water known as zooplankton. When coral polyps feed, extending their fingerlets from their calcium carbonate home, called a theca, they appear as many wands waving to an unheard music, orchestrating the food into the animals' oral cavity.

The study of fossil evidence has determined that coral reefs on earth were destroyed at least twice over history, and perhaps as many as four times. With the collapse of the coral reef communities, the entire face of the Earth changed and many species of life became extinct.

The most recent collapse of the reef community is said to have occurred in the late Cretaceous period, about sixty-five million years ago. The great dinosaurs which then roamed the Earth died out. The Earth's cores welled up in volcanoes, and the basins of the seas were created. During this part of the Cretaceous period, one-third of all animals on earth became extinct, and probably two-thirds of the coral families were also extinguished. The basins that were created caused the water to drain off vast areas of the land, which were now left high and dry. This explains why marine fossils can be found today in high reaches of certain mountain ranges.

In the Malay Archipelago, for example, coral formations have been found in fossil evidence four thousand feet above sea level, and nicknamed by geologists "the Atolls on Mountains."

During the Cenozoic era, some twenty million years ago, the Earth's temperature was dramatically changed by the creation of the polar ice caps. Currents changed in the oceans and coral was killed by the cold polar water or forced into the tropical oceans. In the warm tropical waters, coral species established themselves, building upon rocks, obstructions, and upwelled stone from the Earth's core, forming the coral reefs that we know today.

The survival of coral reefs is directly linked to the survival of vast numbers of other plant and animal species—even human survival. For all of its immensity, the coral reef community is relatively fragile, depending on a clean, pollution-free environment.

Today, coral reefs are in peril. While destruction will

not take place overnight and only rarely over short periods, the continual degradation of the marine environment in many parts of the world by industrial and human pollution, construction and silting over, is taking a serious toll.

Most everyone has seen examples of coral breakage. Any snorkler over tropical reefs has seen broken coral heads and branches, the result of careless boat anchoring. If this happened only once, or infrequently, it would not be very serious. New coral growth would replace broken areas. However, in some tropical areas, reefs have been destroyed by repeated careless anchoring. The problem has become so serious in some places, like on Bonaire, that rules have been passed to require that boats tie up only at buoyed-off anchorages where permanent moorings have been installed.

Most everyone has observed dried and bleached coral for sale in novelty stores and shell shops—even from roadside stands in tropical regions. This coral, while ornamental and popular to display in the home, has been broken off living reefs. Often the islanders, whose lives depend on the reefs since they support the fish consumed for food, will destroy the coral to sell chunks of it to tourists. This destruction creates a short-term financial benefit, since tourists pay a lot for the coral trinkets and souvenirs, adding to the island economy. Sometimes islanders use coral from the reefs to build walls, roads, or houses. In the long run, however, the destruction of the reef dooms the islanders to poverty, for in addition to tourism decreasing with the diminishing beauty of an island's reefs, the habitat of fish and shellfish will be destroyed as well, decreasing the inhabitants' ability to subsist.

Construction near the water or the dumping of construction debris into the water has also caused vast destruction of coral reefs. Dredging for the construction of boat channels or for building causes a great deal of silt in the water. Not only does the silt cover the reef, choking the coral polyps

Dead coral; a reef devastated by pollution and physical breakage.

and, in extreme cases, killing them, but the construction dumping and dredging causes a change in water clarity that prevents sunlight from penetrating to the reef. Sunlight is a necessary ingredient for coral growth.

It was only relatively recently that the relationship between light and coral growth was explained scientifically. It was found that marine algae, microscopic plants, live inside coral polyps. These algae are called zooxanthellae. The zooxanthellae use the carbon dioxide, sulfur, phosphorus, and nitrogen that is produced as waste by the coral to manufacture starch. This increases the coral's energy-saving ability, since it does not have to excrete the wastes. This saving of energy is converted into the construction of the coral's limestone skeleton, the theca.

All plants require light. The more light there is, the more oxygen is produced by these coral algae, which are plants, and the more efficiently they convert the waste generated by the coral. Without light, the zooxanthellae die. While experiments are still being conducted to determine the extent to which these marine plants aid coral growth, it is known that where coral was placed in a box without light and the algae died, coral growth decreased markedly. Coral was found to grow ten times faster in light than in the dark, clear evidence of the importance of these microscopic algae. This explains the flourishing growth of coral near the surface of the ocean, where plenty of sunlight penetrates.

Thus, if the clarity of the water is affected and the amount of sunlight reaching the coral is decreased, coral growth will decrease as well.

However, some forms of coral grow at extreme depths, often in subdued light. Red Mediterranean coral is found at such depths, for it is a hard and dense coral with a very slow growth rate. Ancient Egyptians treasured red coral, and biblical writings describe it. It is valued for jewelry, and branches

True red coral is found only in the Mediterranean. It is prized for jewelry and decorative use. Large branches like this one have more value than gold when sold by weight.

of it that once grew in shallower water have long since been taken by coral divers. The desirability of red coral has accounted for its overharvesting and scarcity.

In tropical areas, other varieties of coral have been depleted as well, resulting in diminished life around the reef. Hard rose coral is harvested commercially by minisubmarines at extreme depths off the Hawaiian islands. The coral is polished and made into jewelry for sale on the island of Oahu.

THE USE of dynamite and explosives to catch fish has also caused vast destruction of coral reefs around the world. Dynamite fishing is wasteful. Far more fish die and sink to the bottom than float to the surface or swim within reach of the fishermen. The use of explosives destroys the reef below, killing coral that has taken centuries to grow. In turn, the habitat of the fish is destroyed, and the fish disappear.

In the remote islands of Micronesia in the South Pacific, local divers found a bounty of explosives inside sunken Japanese warships. This enterprising group of brigands recovered bombs from the sunken wrecks, then cut them open and used the explosives inside to make smaller bombs. They used these to dynamite-fish the reefs around the islands, and the devastation was extreme. The efficiency of this unlawful operation was increased by the fact that the men used scuba tanks to recover fish that were killed and sank to the bottom. Vast reaches of coral reefs were in danger of destruction from this one group. Eventually, the men's own carelessness and not the law put an end to their activities, when one of the divers, smoking a cigarette near where the others were cutting a bomb in half, blew the operation to smithereens.

Still, dynamite fishing goes on in remote areas of the world where ignorance and poverty make it tempting. It is especially important to educate the people in these regions

A parrot fish nibbling at coral. When the fish excrete the coral through their digestive systems, it forms coral sand, eventually becoming part of the beach.

that destruction of the reefs destroys the food supply, since their lives depend on food from the sea.

Of course, not all coral damage is caused by humans. Storms and hurricanes also account for the breaking of coral and the destruction of reefs. Reefs surrounding islands act as barriers to storms, protecting the homes of inhabitants. Without the fringing reefs and barrier reefs, many tropical islands would be destroyed by the pounding ocean and storms.

Certain animals also account for coral damage. Trigger fish and parrot fish are notorious coral nibblers. Their strong

The crown of thorns starfish, a menace to the reef, grazing over living coral.

beaks munch away at living corals, and they leave behind them a trail of waste droppings. This waste—the digested grains of calcium carbonate, the limestone skeletons of the coral—becomes sand, creating coral sand beaches. Predation by these and other fish and marine animals is part of a natural balance that maintains the stability of a tropical reef population.

Another natural enemy of coral is the crown of thorns starfish. This ravenous denizen of the deep eats living coral polyps. When present in large numbers, starfish can destroy vast amounts of coral. It is thought that the disappearance of the sea creature Triton's Trumpet, whose beautiful shell is often seen in movies about Polynesia, has upset the balance in nature in these reefs and allowed the starfish to get out of control.

The Triton shell, which can be blown if the sharp end is cut off, produces a deep, throaty noise that can echo across an island. The Triton has been collected in large numbers by souvenir hunters and shell fanciers, who quickly depleted the population of these beautiful creatures on the reefs surrounding Polynesia and elsewhere. It is said that the Triton, a natural enemy of the crown of thorns, kept the predatory starfish in check. The theory is valid, for where this natural enemy of the crown of thorns disappeared, starfish populations increased and so did the damage they did to the coral reefs. It is difficult to know precisely what role the Triton played in the control of the crown of thorns, because by the time the relationship was studied, so many shells had been taken from the wild by collectors that their former effect in starfish control could only be guessed.

A stand of staghorn coral growing in shallow water.

CORAL takes many forms. Soft coral, such as gorgonian, attached to the reef by its base, freely bends with the tides and currents. On closer examination, small coral polyps can be observed. The polyps may come out only when the surrounding water is calm, often extending their tentacles to feed at night. Brain coral, when seen during the day, resembles the convolutions of the surface of the brain: thus its name. At night, the brain coral's polyps extend for feeding, and a diver observing them gets a different impression, since the soft tentacles literally cover the entire coral head with fingerlets of color. Staghorn and elkhorn coral are shallow-water corals, growing up in "racks" near the surface.

Science still knows relatively little about the growth rate of coral. Staghorn coral grows about two inches per year, while the dense brain coral increases overall about one-fifteenth of an inch per year. Corallum rubrum, the dense red Mediterranean coral we've described, the only true red coral, is said to add only one centimeter to its growth in every hundred years. Red coral is more valuable by weight than gold, so highly prized are its thick branches in jewelry making.

The interdependence of life on a coral reef is evident to anyone who has taken the time to look. Floating on one's stomach and looking down at a reef through a dive mask, or donning scuba equipment and spending time underwater exploring, convinces us of the beauty, the majesty of the coral reef. There is evidence everywhere of the destruction of coral by its worst enemy, humans. The survival of coral reefs around the world directly affect the lives of millions of people. Fish and marine life depend on coral: as shelter, as breeding grounds where they can lay their eggs, and to provide food and homes for the food the fish eat. Without the reef, these creatures will decrease or disappear. For all of us, protection and conservation of coral reefs means survival.

4

Killers Where the Sea Lives

THEY WERE tough kids. In New York's Central Park Zoo, anyone observing their rowdy behavior could tell the youths were looking for trouble. The Central Park Zoo used to house large animals in the middle of Manhattan, in closely confined, cruel conditions. Regal tigers and great apes rubbed themselves raw against the bars of their small cages, bored, sentenced to a life of stress. Inside the zoo buildings, visitors would yell, taunt the animals, and throw junk food into their cages. Grand and magnificent animals were displayed as freaks. Outside, the zoo kept sea lions in a pool. They would swim and dive and climb up on the concrete borders. The pool was small, yet the sea lions cavorted and played among themselves.

The group of young toughs emerged from a zoo building and headed for the sea lion pool. There were no keepers present, as there had been inside the buildings, where the rowdies had tried to throw things at the animals in the cages.

The youths first jeered and gestured at the sea lions. Then, not satisfied, unchecked by guards or zookeepers, they emptied the contents of a trash basket and began throwing bottles and debris at the animals. A person who tried to interfere was threatened. By the time onlookers could get help, the urban toughs had run off.

A zookeeper who appeared told of zoos finding fishhooks and glass in the stomachs of sea lions that had died. Apparently, some cruel person had purposely imbedded these items inside food thrown to the animals. The unfortunate creatures had died a tortured death, as the broken glass and fishhooks tore into their stomachs and intestines.

Anyone who thinks that human interference with wild animals is unimportant or insignificant need only consider the case of the plains buffalo, which no longer runs in vast numbers. Hunting this animal used to be great sport. Brave hunters would fire guns out of the windows of trains that had stopped expressly for the killing, until huge herds were exterminated and the fields and plains ran red with blood. Then the trains would push on, leaving the dead animals to rot.

Cruelty to animals may be somewhat more sophisticated in today's world, although the deliberate slaughter of dolphins in Japan, of whales hunted to the verge of extinction, and of fur seals and seal pups clubbed to death on the ice is hardly sophisticated cruelty. Just as cruel is the practice of trapping great sea animals like the orca, or other marine mammals, to imprison them in confined aquariums for human entertainment.

The problem of killing nearly extinct and endangered marine animals for food or adornment is not easily solved. Even more complicated is the issue of confining large marine mammals for research or entertainment. Humans derive educational value from aquariums. In many cases, contact with marine mammals in captivity goes a long way toward raising the level of consciousness about the plight of these animals in the wild. But humans have become killers and trappers on a scale never before imagined possible.

The Native American with bow and arrow could scarcely do the harm to buffalo herds that great numbers of shooters with repeating rifles could and did do. No more buffalo, no more Native Americans. They starved and they froze for want of the food, clothing, and shelter made from buffalo meat and hides. But what about marine mammals, those warm-blooded sea creatures that nurture their young with milk, as humans do, and possess great intelligence. Will our lives be diminished by their passing? We will explore some of these issues as we consider the plight of creatures in the oceans.

NORINE Rouse began scuba diving after raising two daughters, at a time of life when one's leisure activities usually center around entertainment. Not Norine. Once she discovered the marvels of the underwater world, she decided that she would pursue a whole new career around the sea. Norine trained and became a certified scuba diving instructor, working first in the Bahamas and then moving to South Florida, where she settled in Palm Beach County.

Norine opened a small dive shop on Singer Island and began taking divers out to reefs in the Atlantic Ocean where they could dive in the flow of the Gulf Stream. Norine called it drift diving. Once overside, the divers could be carried along underwater, drifting with the swift-flowing current, while a float at the surface enabled her pilot, navigating the dive boat above, to follow them. The fast-flowing current was exhilirating, as were the large and wondrous sea creatures that befriended and were befriended by Norine.

Little by little Norine was accepted by the creatures inhabiting the reefs. Little by little Norine accepted them, too, until this aquanaut was as much at home on the ocean floor as she was in her living room or driving her car. She fed and tamed large moray eels and immense groupers called Jew-

*Conservationist Norine Rouse putting an end to another
speargun. Norine has battled for ocean conservation for years
and only now, when great harm has already been done, are
people beginning to realize that Norine was right when she
warned that the reefs off Florida's Atlantic coast were menaced
by abuse and the emptying of canal water from the interior.*

fish. She cavorted with aged sea turtles, some probably eighty or a hundred years old.

Other divers in Florida fished with spear guns and bang-sticks, spears carrying an explosive head that kills on impact. But Norine was different. She learned the habits of marine creatures and took on a responsibility for trying to preserve the reefs, which provided not only her daily livelihood but also her inspiration.

One day, when seeking out a very large moray eel she had befriended, bringing down food each time she ventured by the moray's home on the reef, Norine came upon the handiwork of human cruelty. A spearfisherman had impaled the tame moray and left it to die on the reef. It was not killed for food—not even for a trophy. It was killed just because it was there. The animal had been tamed by Norine and came to expect food each time it heard the reassuring sound of divers' bubbles. The trusting animal had ventured forth and met death at the hands of a human killer in the deep.

From that moment on, Norine made two resolutions. She would no longer feed and tame wild animals, making them easy targets for spearfishermen, and she would no longer permit spear guns on any of her dive trips. Norine also offered a reward: She would give a free dive trip to anyone who brought in a spear gun and permitted her to bend it over her knee.

Over the next few years Norine earned a reputation all along Florida's coast. She became known as "that conservationist lady," or "that spear gun lady," as she defended the rights of marine animals in the wild and developed bruised knees and shins bending hundreds of spear guns. The pile of bent spears grew and grew, and eventually Norine's pleas were heard. Today, thanks to the efforts of Norine and divers like her, many areas of the Atlantic off Palm Beach County's

A marine turtle in the Atlantic showing boring barnacles on its carapace or shell. These boring barnacles can cause death to marine turtles, a concern Norine Rouse has undertaken to correct, diving with a pot scrubber and small knife to help her marine turtle friends.

coastline are declared marine sanctuaries, where spearfishing is outlawed.

Sea turtles, large air-breathing reptiles, show up off Palm Beach every winter. Norine noticed that the same turtles kept coming back to the reef year after year, and she began observing them. Marine turtles are considered an endangered species and are protected by law. They cannot be hunted or killed, their nests, dug on sand beaches, cannot be disturbed, and trafficking in turtle products—their flesh, their shells or items made from them, or calipee, the cartilage attached to the lower shell that is valued for turtle soup—is unlawful in the United States.

Norine Rouse with an officer of the Florida Marine Patrol with a turtle she had just rescued from the surf. It was too late for this animal, which eventually died at the animal refuge.

Even with the protective laws, Norine and her divers continued to observe acts of cruelty against these endangered animals. Turtles were found with gunshot wounds, the victims of boaters who fired at them when they came to the surface to breathe.

Norine also discovered natural problems that were claiming the lives of many turtles as well. "These boring barnacles eat right through the turtles' shells," she noted, and began taking a small knife and a pot-scrubber pad with her on dives, to remove boring barnacles from the shells of her friends. On one occasion, a diver Norine had trained telephoned that a turtle was stranded on one of the beaches. Norine jumped in her car and went directly to the beach, where an obviously weak sea turtle was struggling in the surf. Norine helped bring the turtle up on the sand, and she and a volunteer with a truck transported the sick animal to a refuge farther up the coast. The turtle later died, and the cause of death was found to be boring barnacles, which had drilled into the animal's head.

"That may be one reason why the turtles burrow into the thick mud that has come out of the canals," Norine observed. "Down in that thick ooze there is no oxygen, and the barnacles die. Many of the older turtles have a lot of barnacles on their heads and necks, and some have large numbers of boring barnacles on their carapace.

"Last month we were diving on the reef and we found a large Hawksbill turtle, very lethargic. We knew it was sick, so we helped it to the surface. On the way up, blood started spewing from the turtle's neck. It had been shot. On the bottom the pressure of the depth had stemmed the flow of blood, but the animal was doomed. We took it aboard the boat to try and get it to the animal refuge, but it died. You have unthinking people in boats out here who kill for no reason," Norine said, obviously fighting back her emotions as she described the sad incident.

Historically turtles have been widely used for food. In the early voyages of discovery, turtles were one of the sailors' few sources of fresh meat. Turtle meat and turtle soup, made from the calipee—even turtle eggs—are considered delicacies by some people. With the disruption in turtle habitats all over the world by the construction of hotels and housing complexes that encroach on wild nesting beaches, by marauding packs of wild dogs and other predatory animals that dig up turtle nests and eat the eggs, by disruption from humans hunting both the turtles and their eggs—with all of these factors, marine turtles worldwide are in danger of disappearing.

A Kodak Pathé newsreel from 1947 shows the arrival of thousands of marine turtles on a beach in Mexico. The mass arrival was called the *arribada*. But in today's world, there are no more *arribadas;* none on this grand scale have been observed for generations. Sea turtles come back to the same beach where they were born to mate and nest after many years at sea. Where they go after nesting and how they are able to navigate hundreds, even thousands of miles to come back to the very same place where they were born is one of those wonderful mysteries of nature that is being solved little by little by the observations of people like Norine Rouse and other concerned turtle researchers.

From the moment of their hatching out of the eggs that had been deposited by the female turtle in sand nests dug on the beach, little turtles are attacked by gulls and sea birds, which devour them in large numbers. Of the hatchlings that do survive, many fall prey in the ocean to sharks and other animals. Turtle eggs are collected for food in Central American countries, so many eggs do not even hatch. Often, on nesting beaches, calipee hunters turn the nesting turtles over and cut off their bottom shells to get at the strips of cartilage, cruelly leaving the animals to suffer, still alive, slowly dying in the sun while their entrails are pecked at by sea birds.

Researchers now believe that the scent of their birthplace

Turtle hatchlings being raised in captivity to be released into the ocean, with the hope of giving them a better chance for survival.

is imprinted on baby turtle hatchlings, which enables them later in life to find their way home to breed and lay their own eggs. Scientists are now attempting to gather up baby turtles that have hatched out on polluted or developed beaches and transport them to protected beaches where they are kept for a while, hoping the new scent will be imprinted, and these turtles, when they return, will come back to a beach where there is a better chance for survival of their offspring.

Trying to satisfy the demand for turtle soup, turtle meat, and products made from turtle shells, a turtle farm was established on the Cayman Islands. Strict laws about trafficking in turtle products, even from raised turtles, has prevented the export of these raised turtle products to the United States.

The turtle farm has also established a program of encouraging tourists to buy turtles, which are then released into the wild. There has been some success with this "sponsoring" of marine turtles, and the foster parents often take great pride in releasing an endangered species into the ocean.

It is difficult to predict the extent to which human interference with sea turtles will affect the future wild population of this endangered animal. With careful vigilance and strict enforcement of the laws protecting these large marine reptiles, perhaps turtles will be saved from extinction.

SLOW—MANATEE AREA large signs proclaim, posted in the boat channel along Florida's Intracoastal Waterway. An endangered species, pushed nearly to the verge of extinction, the manatee, or sea cow, has been menaced by human encroachment, taunted by cruel boaters, and often cut apart by negligently operated speedboats in Florida's inland waterways.

Manatees are warm-blooded creatures belonging to the order *Sirenia*. They are thought to be the "mermaids" described by sailors, though they are hardly anyone's idea of a sleek siren or mermaid. Sailors who thought so must have been at sea a long time.

These gentle creatures are vegetarians and browse on sea grasses and plants such as water hyacinth in lakes and springs and along Florida's coastal waters. Other kinds of manatees, called dugongs, live in rivers around the world. Manatees have valves that can close over their nostrils when they dive for food. They often remain submerged for several minutes before surfacing to breathe.

Very little is really known about these animals. Some have lived in captivity for thirty years, but even so, their life span in the wild remains a mystery. The best information on the manatees' reproductive cycle suggests that the female cannot mate until it is around eight or nine years old and the male almost ten years old. Females usually give birth to only one calf at a time; twins are very rare. The mother carries

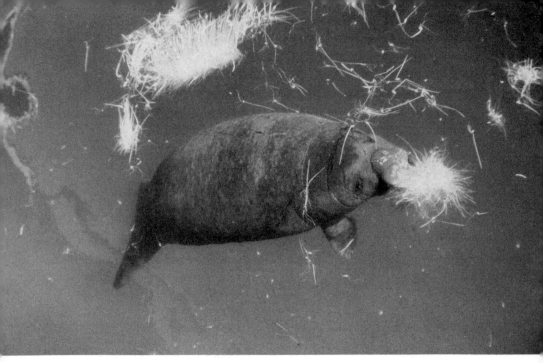

A baby manatee browsing on grasses.

the baby in the womb for a year, then nurses the calf on milk for many weeks. Manatees generally calve only every three to five years, a cycle that has resulted in depletion of the wild populations.

Fossil evidence suggests that manatees evolved about sixty-million years ago, probably from land mammals with four feet. The earliest manatee fossil evidence found in Florida is fourteen million years old. Only vestiges of the forefeet remain on today's manatee, which has two paddlelike front flippers and a large flat tail that propels it through the water.

Florida manatees generally inhabit lakes and springs during summer, browsing on the thick grasses that often obstruct canals and channels, keeping them clear and thereby serving a very useful function. As the water temperature drops in Florida during winter, the animals migrate, entering the Intracoastal Waterway, easily able to tolerate brackish and salt water. Frequently groups of manatees are observed near the out-falls of power plants, where the warm water from the plant's cooling system is discharged. The manatees freely use the Waterway and its inlets to swim between the inland lakes that are their fresh-water habitats and the Atlantic, where they range along the coast.

Manatee populations in Florida have been counted from aircraft. The best counts estimate that there are only between eight hundred and a thousand animals left.

Manatees have no defenses and can protect themselves only by swimming away. But they are relatively slow-moving creatures, and have been slashed by boat propellers as they come to the surface to breathe. Or they are killed while brows-ing on the surface.

Manatees have been protected in Florida for a long time. A 1978 law called the Florida Manatee Sanctuary Act has made the entire state a manatee refuge and sanctuary. Federal laws also protect this endangered species. In spite of protective laws, a study of the cause of manatee deaths revealed that over 30 percent of the 506 dead manatees recovered between 1976 and 1981 were killed by humans or died as a result of human activities. Collisions with boats or boat propellers; death in canal floodgates; inadequate food supply caused by the construction boom throughout Florida, which has de-stroyed the grasses upon which manatees feed; death from fishing hooks and lines; and pollution from insecticides and herbicides, as well as thermal pollution—all these have claimed most victims.

Manatees play a role in controlling weeds and water plants that choke inland lakes and canals, but just as important as this role of the manatee in keeping the balance in nature is their unique place as part of the natural world.

For anyone who has had a chance to glimpse a manatee with its calf swimming in the wild, or browsing peacefully in a lake or stream, it's clear that these creatures, with their sense of gentle harmony, must be allowed to live in peace. Marine aquariums like Miami's Seaquarium have received injured animals and have nursed them back to health. Manatees have, in fact, given birth in captivity, a rare phenomenon. There is some hope that if the population in Florida can be stabilized, these animals might be available for future generations to observe and enjoy: docile creatures in a majestic aquatic world.

CETACEANS are marine mammals such as whales or porpoises, commonly called dolphins. (The mammal dolphin should not be confused with the fish also called a dolphin.) While most of our attention has been focused on the depletion of whale populations in the wild by whaling interests, who have reduced some species of these leviathans of the deep to a population of only a few thousand, another important issue

Deep scars on this manatee's back show that it was run over by the propeller of a power boat.

is the taking of large marine mammals from wild populations for the purpose of confining them in aquariums or seaquarium zoos. Many of these aquariums are poorly maintained, badly run animal freak shows, in which large mammals, such as 14,000-pound killer whales, are confined in small tanks, decked out in silly costumes to amuse paying guests.

Since 1972, a federal law in the United States has required people to get permits in order to take marine mammals from the wild. A recent application was made to capture as many as a hundred killer whales, or orca, by a California-based aquarium. Next to the human being, the orca is the most intelligent animal on earth, even more intelligent than the larger apes. When this application was made public, the outrage of concerned citizens echoed through the halls of the permit agency in Washington. Eventually the permit was denied.

However, seaquariums can serve an important educational function. If the animals are kept under conditions that give them sufficient freedom, and if public shows are done with dignity and offer information about the animals, then visitors will leave with a better understanding of the plight of marine mammals in the wild and an appreciation for their intelligence.

It is often unnecessary to capture animals from wild populations for seaquarium exhibits. Many dolphins and smaller whales that became stranded and were rescued have adapted to the aquarium environment. Also, aquarium animals do mate in captivity, making it unnecessary to take large marine mammals from the wild.

No one can see a killer whale in captivity, learn about the animal's keen intelligence, admire its beauty and grace in the water—no one can do this and not insist that the animal would be better off in the wild. Even those closest to these large marine mammals, their keepers, trainers, and those who run the large seaquariums, feel in their hearts that these large and wondrous creatures ought to be left alone to live out their lives in the wild, protected from human marauders.

WHILE the average person has less qualms about capturing tropical fish and keeping them in home aquariums, the industry involved with the capture and sale of tropical fish has been responsible for the depletion of whole reef colonies. In far-off reaches of the Earth, where tropical fish add color to the reef, collectors use drugs to dope the fish, making them easier to capture. Often whole coral heads are removed from the reef so that the fish that seek refuge within the coral can be taken. Few captured fish survive the use of drugs, the time in holding tanks, and transportation over thousands of miles to aquarium suppliers in the United States and elsewhere, so many more have to be caught than are needed.

Again human greed has come into play, resulting in the destruction of fragile tropical reef environments. While keeping marine animals in tanks may be interesting, all of us must consider the individual benefit against the overall harm done to our marine ecosystems.

An example of the folly of capturing tropical reef fish was evident on the Tahitian island of Moorea, when the owners of a resort there decided to construct a salt-water aquarium. They couldn't be coaxed out of the idea, even by those who said that the visitors to the resort could easily see the same fish by going out in the resort's glass-bottomed boat. Just a few feet from the resort's dock, a small tropical reef had large coral heads that came up near the surface, where the fish swam about in their natural surroundings, unhampered by glass or walls.

The resort owners went ahead with their plans for an aquarium. They built a large glass tank, then had divers go down and take up huge chunks of living coral. They captured the tropical fish that lived on the reef in front of the resort's dock.

After the aquarium was set up, the water in the tank became polluted within a few hours, in spite of the use of filters and pumps. The mix of coral and other marine life was wrong. All the fish died, and the coral had to be thrown out. The resort kept trying, each time breaking up more of the natural reef snorklers once enjoyed and which visitors could have easily seen from a glass-bottomed boat. By the time the aquarium was completed, the entire nearby natural reef was demolished. The resort kept the aquarium in operation for about six months, until the management changed; then it was abandoned, the contents dumped out. While few people ever enjoyed the aquarium, the many people who would have enjoyed the natural reef were cheated, and an ecosystem in the lagoon was destroyed.

Very often, making and keeping a home aquarium is a gimmick or passing fancy. The fish die or are eventually thrown out when people get tired of taking care of them. There are ample public aquariums where visitors can learn about fish. But the best aquarium in the world is right in the seas and oceans, as easy to see as putting on a face mask and snorkle, diving or floating on one's stomach, looking down at the marine life below.

EDUCATING young people about the oceans: that is what a small museum called North Wind is all about. Located on City Island, New York, the museum has a tugboat sticking out of the front of the building, and young visitors are encouraged to walk into the wheelhouse and touch anything they have a mind to. The exhibits include a model of a sperm whale that the North Wind Whale Rescue Team saved when the animal became disoriented and stranded in the waters of Long Island, New York. A film about the rescue of the whale

Kids learn about ocean conservation at North Wind Museum, an institute founded by Michael Sandlofer to teach young people about the importance of protecting the sea.

shows the development of whale harnesses and other rescue equipment, teaching the young viewer about what is being done to protect these animals in the wild.

Young people at North Wind are made aware of the plight of endangered whales while they view a collection of scrimshaw carvings that traces the history of whaling. The scrimshaw was engraved on whale bones and teeth by sailors during their long voyages. Under federal law, the import and sale of whale products is restricted; North Wind's antique collection is displayed under permit.

Whales are the largest of the marine mammals. Some

species, like the blue whale, can grow to a length of more than one hundred feet and weigh as much as one hundred twenty tons. Yet these great leviathans of the deep are very gentle creatures.

Swimming with whales, divers are amazed at their grace and beauty. Humans who have encountered whales while diving have told wonderful stories about how gentle they are, how a whale deliberately swims so as not to hurt the divers with its tail or fluke. Yet these gentle giants have been hunted nearly to extinction.

In 1860, the harpoon cannon and the exploding harpoon were invented, increasing the whaler's deadly accuracy. By 1925, whaling factory ships were introduced, huge vessels with slipways big enough to haul a whole animal aboard for processing. Accompanied by fleets of fast-killing catching

Michael Sandlofer and the crew of North Wind Museum have been testing and developing whale rescue gear, hoping to be able to free stranded and beached whales. Here the North Wind rescue team has found a dead whale carcass and is trying out the equipment.

*Off the coast of Lanai in the Hawaiian islands, whales frolic
in the Pacific. Their songs can be heard for miles. Here a
whale breaches, jumping high out of the water and falling
back with a great splash and noise. Some theorize that the
whale is trying to rid itself of attaching organisms, others feel
it is just a way whales play.*

boats firing harpoon cannons, each factory ship churned the
oceans of the world red with whale blood.

By the 1930–31 whaling season, there were forty-one
factory ships with two hundred catching boats prowling the
Antarctic waters, the last refuge of these gentle giants. In
the 1930–31 whaling season alone, a total of 37,465 whales
were taken. Of this total, 28,325 blue whales were killed,
not counting those wounded, escaping in agony only to die
later in the deep.

By 1946, whaling nations sent representatives to take part in International Whaling Convention meetings. The results of these meetings produced a major disaster for the world whale population. Quotas were established in Blue Whale Units (blues are the largest of the whales). Each Blue Whale Unit was equal to 6 sei whales or 2 fin whales or 2½ humpbacks. The quota system thus targeted the blues as the most desirable catch, causing further depletion of this endangered species. Blue Whale Unit quotas were stopped in 1972, but by then it was almost too late. From an estimated average world population of 33,000 blue whales during the years 1933 to 1939, only 1,000 to 3,000 were left by 1963. Even fewer blue whales are left today, and many other species of whale have joined them on the endangered list.

However, it is not only the concern of conservationists that has decreased commercial whaling. Ironically, the whaling interests hunted whales to the verge of extinction at a time when the world markets for whale oil and whale products, such as corset stays, declined, making whaling unprofitable.

HUMAN KILLERS in the sea have done great damage to nature. We must learn to appreciate the intelligence, beauty, and purpose of the other creatures that inhabit this planet, and we must insure their protection.

Sharks are much maligned creatures of the deep. They play an important role in nature and must not be killed for sport or out of ignorance and fear.

5

Sharks, Hunters of the Deep

FEAR and misinformation surround sharks and shark behavior. Sharks kill; that is how they live. They are large, predatory animals. Sharks also devour garbage, and dead and diseased or weak animals in the oceans, performing an important function in keeping a balance in nature's ocean world.

After the popular film *Jaws,* screams of fear emanated from beachgoers every time someone imagined they saw something in the water. Tournament fishing for sharks became great sport, and sharks were slaughtered by the thousands.

Killing anything for sport is unsporting in a world beset by hunger. In the ocean realm, where everything has its place, it is particularly foolish to destroy animals simply because they are little understood or because humans have fears or superstitions about them. It is plainly wrong to thrill at the killing of animals such as sharks, large and venerable creatures of the deep.

Sharks *can* be dangerous to humans, just as all wild creatures can be dangerous when circumstances place them in contact with potential prey. It is probably no surprise to anyone that the number of shark attacks on people each year is even less than the number of people who are struck by lightning. Yet because both incidents are rare and can cause grave and blood-chilling consequences, the press and television blow the incidents up with great publicity giving macabre details.

Yet some people have a completely different point of view. Here's how John Stoneman, one of the world's best-known underwater filmmakers and naturalists, described a shark hunt: "They killed them all. If you can imagine it. He told them to kill one shark, which was bad enough, but the divers went down and killed all of the sharks. All of them. We were studying this group of territorial reef sharks in the Bahamas. And they just killed them all . . ." Stoneman's voice trailed off, dejected, his British accent still strong even after many years living in Canada.

The sadness Stoneman feels is surprising to some people. Why should he feel sad that a population of sharks was slaughtered? In his dramatic television films, sharks are shown swimming in a feeding frenzy, ripping speared fish off the ends of harpoons, making menacing passes at divers, endangering the lives of the filmmakers below. Why then would John Stoneman or anyone else who had witnessed the potential danger and violent behavior of sharks firsthand have any sympathy for letting them live?

"Very little is really known about the group behavior of sharks," Stoneman explained. "In fact, the territorial nature of this one group was just giving us some insight into their importance to the life of the reef community." He knew that his research on this aspect of shark behavior would never be completed because of the intervention of human killers, who for no valid purpose destroyed a population of animals even before their importance could be assessed.

The senseless acts described by John Stoneman are not rare. Human killers seem lured by the thrill of killing. To many of them, it is "macho" to risk danger and destroy, without mercy, creatures in nature.

While filming in the remote Tuamotu Islands in French Polynesia, I learned from the Tahitian people on the island of Rangiroa how hundreds of sharks could be summoned in front of the camera within moments, either by simulating the sound and vibrations of wounded fish by rattling a string of coconut shells, or by actually spearing a fish underwater. Living with sharks is a way of life on Rangiroa, and the people take them in stride. Polynesians spear fish for their daily food and thus depend on the ocean for life itself. Mauri and Mamaru are their names for black- and white-tip sharks.

Occasionally, a local spearfisherman on Rangiroa is attacked by a shark. One older man bore a deep half-moon scar on his calf, where a shark had bitten him while he was out on the reef, spearing fish. The shark, frenzied by speared fish in the water, mistook the fisherman's leg for prey.

Fishermen know that they have to get their speared fish out of the water as quickly as possible so that sharks are not attracted to the wounded fish's vibrations or to the scent of blood in the water. The fishermen do not kill the sharks, since there is no purpose to it. The islanders do not eat shark meat, preferring instead bonito and other species of fish plentiful on the reefs.

With the advent of scheduled air service from Papeete on the main island of Tahiti, tourists began discovering Rangiroa. With the tourists came the developers, who built a modern hotel on the island. Islanders found they could sell handcrafts and souvenirs to the foreign visitors, so they broke coral from the reefs, dried it, and offered it for sale. They harvested shells in great numbers and sold them to the tourists. Local divers found that there was a profitable market for shark jaws, so they began slaughtering sharks for the sole purpose of cutting away their jaws to dry and sell.

The reef life on Rangiroa suffered. Spearing for sport was taken up by tourists and encouraged by local guides, who stood to make a profit taking visitors out in their boats. It wasn't really very sporting; their pneumatic spear guns could kill with certainty virtually anything they struck. It was almost like shooting fish in a barrel, since marine life was so abundant on the reefs.

Spearfishing got out of hand. The manager of the hotel saw clearly that if the spearing continued, the magnificent reefs the tourists came to see would soon be destroyed. If the reefs were destroyed, his investment in the hotel would be of little value. So he had small cards printed in English and French and posted them in the guests' rooms. They read: "It takes ten years for a fish to grow, only a second to kill it. Don't be trigger happy."

Local divers on Rangiroa continue and will continue to kill sharks for their jaws as long as unthinking tourists continue to create a market for them. That is the way of things. Human greed is the same all over the world. As with the thrill killing of animals for sport, there is a part of human nature that can be conquered only by education. Humans must learn that everything has its place in nature and there is a place for everything.

Sharks evolved some hundred million years ago. Their skeletons are composed entirely of cartilage—no bone at all, which means shark bodies are very fragile. Sharkskin is very rough; it can rub the skin off a diver's or fisherman's hand. In some places of the world, sharkskin is used as sandpaper.

On the island of Rangiroa in French Polynesia, divers kill sharks to sell their jaws to tourists. It is easy enough to enforce conservation measures if educated tourists resist the temptation to purchase shark souvenirs.

When sharks are attacked by pods of dolphins—in nature, one of the few enemies of sharks—the dolphins butt the sharks with their hard muzzles. As a result the sharks bleed internally and die. Frequently sharks hooked on fishing lines for sport and then released also die, because the fight they put up damages their internal organs, unprotected by the bony skeleton other fish have.

Sharks are more closely related to stingrays, mantas, and skates, which also have cartilage skeletons, than they are to other fish. They reproduce sexually and, depending on species, bear their young in different ways. Some species lay eggs oviparously, in pods or sacs that hatch in time; others, like the hammerhead or white-tip, bear their young viviparously, with the baby sharks growing in the female's womb, or ovoviviparously (mako or thresher sharks), with the young hatched inside the female's body and released when mature.

One aspect of shark behavior was seen off the Polynesian island of Moorea. A pod of whales was sighted outside the reef by a group of divers I was with on a boat in fairly deep water. I jumped into the water ahead of the whales, camera in hand, in what would prove to be a special adventure. Moments after I reached the pod of whales, the Tahitian captain on the boat began calling and waving his arms. The pod of whales was being shadowed by large, oceanic white-tip sharks. The sharks kept their distance, circling the whales, hoping to attack a weak calf or to feed on the afterbirth from a calving female.

Another diver from the boat, grabbed a spear gun and jumped into the water, but it was foolish to think that a spear gun used amid a hundred or more sharks would do anything but provoke a frenzy among the animals. The diver with the spear gun was signaled back to the boat. As he retreated in fear, the sharks approached. Seeing the sharks come closer, the diver with the spear gun swam quickly, pan-

Mummified sharks and rays for sale to tourists along the Red Sea coast in Egypt. If tourists refuse to buy such souvenirs, then senseless killing will stop.

icked now, afraid they were going to attack him. His erratic swimming pattern caused the sharks to draw even closer. See-ing the sharks approach underwater, I put aside my camera-work and, with bold, deliberate movements, swam toward the large oceanic sharks. These oceanics were nothing like the white-tip reef sharks; they were larger—about ten feet long—and were hunting for a meal. I fired the camera's under-water strobe light and the closest of the sharks sped away. This enabled us to regain the safety of the ship.

These sharks were hunting to survive. There was nothing cruel in their selection of food; the animals behave instinc-tively, hunting in the easiest manner available to them. If there had been afterbirth, they would have devoured it; if a whale calf had been born sick or weak, or if a member of the whale pod had been injured or weakened by illness, then it would have fallen prey to the sharks. The human presence was no part of the equation of shark survival in the ocean. It was a chance encounter.

Sharks behave in ways that can be understood only in terms of their need to survive. Their conduct has no ven-geance, premeditated cruelty, or formed thought, other than the thought processes motivated by the primitive instincts to find food and to reproduce.

As part of that natural equation, these predators of the deep cull animals from the wild population. Creatures in the wild survive only if they are fit; if not, they fall prey to preda-tors, which perform the important task of seeing to it that the species itself survives. If the weak and unfit—sick or de-formed—creatures in the ocean environment continue to re-produce, then the species as a whole will be weakened, both in competition for available food and through reproduction, where genes of unfit organisms continue in the natural popula-tion.

If sharks were eliminated, then the natural balance that

exists in nature would be upset. In time, overpopulation of the natural prey of sharks would create yet another imbalance—perhaps the overharvesting of the prey's food. Assuming the toothed whales swimming off Moorea favored the Tahitian staple of bonito, then humans would go hungry.

Problems arising from the destruction of predator-prey relationships in nature are not readily apparent. It may require years before any effect can be seen. There have been ample experiences on land of imbalances caused by humans. In areas where coyotes, wolves, or mountain lions are hunted—where humans consider them pests or fear them or consider it sport to kill them—there is a resulting proliferation of wild deer, a natural prey of these predators. The expanded population of wild deer then overgrazes their range, descending in large numbers to feed off domestic farm crops. In response to the overpopulation of deer, humans take up their guns again and begin killing them. Deer populations that have overgrazed their forage areas also die in large numbers over winter, when there is even less to eat. All of this for the lack of a little common sense.

Creatures in nature survived in the wild long before human interference. Only in the last hundred years or so has the human population become so large and our technology so developed that this human interference has been possible at all. Now people have settled even the last of the terrestrial wilderness, destroying the forest habitats of wild animals.

In the oceans there still remains a vast and uncharted wilderness. It is to be hoped that we can learn from our mistakes on land and not destroy animals simply because they are there, because they are large, because we may fear them, or because those fears may sometimes be justified when chance encounters produce dramatic attacks.

Sharks are magnificent creatures to observe in the ocean, where there are some 250 different species. Some, such as

Just after the author took this picture of a shark swimming in the Pacific off the island of Moorea, it ducked under a coral head. For the most part sharks are timid and photographers have a difficult time getting good pictures underwater.

whale sharks, which grow to sixty feet in length, are filter feeders like baleen whales, eating small plant and animal organisms, or plankton. Some sharks are no more than six inches long.

Sharks are also eaten by humans, and those who have acquired a taste for shark fin soup or shark meat find it quite palatable. It may be that human survival will one day be directly linked to the shark as a form of food, as many more popular species of fish disappear through overfishing and pollution.

The craze to kill—to brand as a worthless menace animals having an important role in nature—is human arrogance. As our planet shrinks, as species disappear even before their role and importance in nature can be fully understood, we cannot permit this arrogance. For the shark, as with any creature in nature, human interference and intervention should occur only when there is a sound reason based on our own need for food or survival. And then, it must be intelligent interference, with sound practices to insure that sharks continue to live in the ocean realm as nature intended.

A ferocious killer of the deep. It would appear so, until the reader is told that this is a frozen shark, caught by line fishermen and put back in the ocean by the author so that he could simulate shark action for a film. Everything has a place in nature, and the menacing shark behavior often seen in films about sharks is most often provoked by baiting them or by speared fish creating a feeding frenzy.

6

Toxic Wastes Contamination of the Oceans

THE CREEK ran into the river and the river ran into the ocean. "We called the Federal Environmental Protection Agency," a town councilman said, standing near the creek. He threw up his arms and pointed to the site. "The EPA came. They looked, tested, and told us we have a problem. We knew we had a problem; that's why we called them," the town official added in disgust.

The problem the town official was confronted with held the potential for disaster. Some two hundred to four hundred tons of mercury had been dumped on the ground along the banks of Berry's Creek in a small New Jersey community. The creek ran into the Hackensack River, which runs into Newark Bay and the Atlantic Ocean. The ocean area there is one of the most productive and popular commercial and sport fishing zones on the East Coast. How the mercury waste got there, the potential environmental and health hazards it presented, and the costly, almost impossible task of cleaning it up is but one example of the perplexing problems we face in the potential assault on our ocean resources by contamination from toxic and poisonous wastes. These toxic wastes are dumped—sometimes deliberately, sometimes accidentally, sometimes indirectly—into our valuable water resources. For generations to come, toxic discharges will plague the important food supply we derive from the seas and oceans of the world.

The problem at Berry's Creek had its origins in a mercury-processing plant operating near the waterway. The mercury was used as ballast in early submarines. The plant remained on the site along Berry's Creek from about 1937 until 1973, when the company ceased operations and went out of business. The old factory building was torn down, and a food warehouse was built in its place. What was left behind was years of mercury spillage and mercury-contaminated waste discarded by the plant.

Over the years that the factory had operated on the site, mercury-contaminated waste was just thrown out: thrown on the ground, along the banks of the creek, and into the creek bed itself.

Mercury is the element that contaminated the food supply of a small fishing village in Minamata, Japan, killing animals and poisoning the inhabitants. A paint factory had dumped mercury-contaminated wastes into Minamata Bay, and the poisons were absorbed by sea animals and fish. People who depended on their daily catch of fish and shellfish for food contracted mercury poisoning. Fifty people died in the village. Photographs of horribly deformed children born to mothers who ate the mercury-contaminated fish haunt everyone who has seen them.

At Berry's Creek, the town official said, "We were told the mercury may eventually migrate down into the creek, then into the river, and then into the ocean. The costs of cleaning up this mess are enormous. The town doesn't have

the money. We don't want a tragedy like they had in Minamata," he said.

"We contacted a mercury processor. Mercury is valuable
and expensive. We asked if they would want to take the dirt
from the site and refine it, to get the mercury. They said no.
The mercury-refining company told us that given the two to
four hundred tons of mercury that was potentially there, recov-
ering it would depress the price of mercury so much it would
hurt their business. Can you imagine that? There is so much
mercury on our creek bank that the refiners of mercury won't
touch it because it would affect their price. So what do we
do?" he asked.

That question asked by the New Jersey town official has
been asked over and over by mayors, governors, and high-
ranking officials all over the world. What can be done when
the undisciplined, improper, and often illegal dumping of poisonous and dangerous materials into the environment creates
such a situation? The enormous potential health and environmental danger must be attended to, yet the cost of dealing
with it and lack of technology to cope with the problem creates
a dilemma about what to do and how to do it.

Problems like the mercury in the ground at Berry's Creek,
which remains unsolved, will not go away. And this is one
of the conditions and cases officials actually know about. The
helter-skelter disposal of toxic wastes throughout the world
has caused toxic poisons to enter the environment in many
other, often unknown ways.

Some of the more serious ways these poisons enter our
oceans and water resources occur by direct ocean dumping
of harmful chemicals and wastes; indirect dumping, where
the poisons reach the sea as runoffs from rivers and streams;
and leaching of toxic elements from landfill sites built along
marshlands, harbors, and back bays. Contamination can also
occur from the incineration of wastes, the combustion of in-

Barrels of chemical waste and debris clog the world's water resources. All of this gives us little hope for the future unless we make a concerted effort to clean up the mess we have made and prevent the continued use of the waters of the world as an all-purpose garbage can.

dustrial by-products, even automobile exhaust fumes. All combustion, or burning, vaporizes particles, which then enter the atmosphere. But, eventually the particles fall back to earth, accumulated in raindrops.

The Earth's systems are all interconnected. To alter or change any one of them, even in areas far away from the oceans, will sooner or later have a dramatic effect on the ocean environment.

The North Atlantic trade winds carry dust and sand from as far away as the Sahara Desert in Africa. The Sahara sand is carried thousands of miles, until it falls on Florida, Puerto

Rico, Bermuda, Barbados, and other Caribbean areas. Sahara sand and dust travel farther west with the trade winds and fall to earth in rain, eventually caught up in the winds that blow north in the Gulf of Mexico.

The Sahara sand and dust cause a haze that blocks out some of the sunlight striking the ocean. It is possible that this blocking of the sun would lower the surface temperature of the ocean. With a change in temperature, the kind and pattern of life in the oceans will also change. Thus an alteration in an environment far, far away can affect the ocean in ways we hardly understand.

Widespread drought in the sub-Sahara region known as the Sahel, which forms a belt across Africa's midsection south of the desert, has caused starvation there and in Ethiopia, a country on the Red Sea. These drought conditions are natural events that occur periodically throughout history. The Sahel drought causes increased sand and dust to be carried by the wind into the atmosphere. Thus a drought in Africa, thousands of miles away from the Caribbean island homes of people who depend on the bounty of the sea, is of direct and vital concern to them.

We are all part of the whole. If we are careless about the land, as we have been by overharvesting, overuse, and poor management, we affect the oceans. Where land resources have been depleted, forests stripped of their trees, and watersheds destroyed, we have changed the balance, the equilibrium on earth.

It is an elementary law of physics that nothing is actually destroyed; matter is only changed from one state to another. Burning anything creates fumes or vapors that enter the atmosphere. The particles in these fumes are carried by the winds and will eventually fall back to earth, captured in rain.

One of the effects of nuclear testing in the desert and in the Pacific has been to increase the levels of radioactive particles in the atmosphere. The radioactive dust falls back to earth, and when it falls on pasture lands, cows grazing there eat grass contaminated with radioactivity. The result is a measurable increase in the radioactive content of milk. When humans drink milk, the radioactive material is transferred to their bodies. When radioactivity levels reach those that scientists have determined to be harmful to human health, then birth defects, cancer, and other diseases occur. When radioactive dust falls in the oceans, there is an increased amount of radioactivity in food we take from the water.

IN ONE particularly flagrant case of dumping hazardous materials into the waterways, a group of people, allegedly connected with organized crime, took over an abandoned bulk oil storage site on Staten Island, New York. The site had been abandoned by an oil company because the nine large storage tanks there, each capable of holding one hundred thousand gallons, were no longer safe. They were leaking and in poor repair. The site was located in a federally protected marshland along Arthur Kill, a waterway that flows into the Atlantic, separating Staten Island from New Jersey.

The new operators of the site told authorities that it was to be used to repackage chemicals, but what occurred was something else again. During the many months that detectives and investigators had the abandoned tank farm under surveillance, thousands and thousands of gallons of toxic wastes were trucked into the site. Many of the wastes contained PCBs (polychlorinated biphenyls), substances known to cause cancer and other diseases in humans and birth defects in unborn children. In addition, hospital laboratory wastes, dangerous chemicals, poisons, and radioactive materials were trucked onto the site. The materials were secretly pumped into the marshland and creek as well as dumped directly into the Arthur Kill.

Police aerial surveillance showed the extent of illegal and improper dumping. When investigators and detectives obtained a search warrant and raided the site, a nightmarish collection of toxic poisons was found. The huge hundred-thousand-gallon storage tanks were filled with contaminated waste, and the entire area contained thousands of barrels of dangerous chemicals.

Dumpster roll-off units were found on the site, filled with still-bottoms—solid materials left over in the chemical manufacturing process—along with other solid toxic waste. Those roll-off units were picked up by truck and dumped into landfills, where the poisons would eventually seep out

Barrels of toxic chemicals stored along the Elizabeth River prior to the explosion and fire at Chemical Control Company in Elizabeth, New Jersey. Some of the most deadly and toxic insecticides, bacteriological discards from laboratories, and other dangerous substances were dumped directly into the river and tributaries leading to the Atlantic.

and contaminate the environment. Mixing pits were found with hidden pipes going directly into a creek. Underground pipes that at one time had been used to offload oil tankers docking along the Arthur Kill, when the site was a legal oil storage facility, were also discovered. The pipes were allegedly used secretly to pump toxic wastes directly into the waterway.

When some of the wastes were found to contain radioactive materials, the New York State Department of Environmental Conservation's regional administrator for all of lower New York was contacted by the chief prosecutor to perform tests on the water in Arthur Kill. Downstream from the toxic waste dump site, the state had been planning at the time to build a power station that would draw water from the Arthur Kill to cool the mechanisms. That water would eventually become vaporized, and the vapor would then enter the air and be breathed by people on Staten Island. The problem was of tremendous public importance.

But the regional administrator of the Department of Environmental Conservation refused to have tests performed to determine the level of radioactivity. The chief prosecutor was told that the DEC assumed that suspicions would be confirmed by the tests, and that the waters surrounding Staten Island were indeed radioactive. However, since the regional administrator felt the Department of Environmental Conservation could do nothing about the problem and did not want to panic the public, they would not perform any tests.

The chief prosecutor then obtained the use of a New York City Police launch so that tests could be made by the New York City Health Department. When the water samples were analyzed by New York University Medical School's Department of Environmental Medicine, they were found to contain twice the normal amount of background radiation. The radiation was from tritium, which proved that contamination was not from a natural source. Radioactive materials had been dumped into the Arthur Kill, probably the result of laboratory waste.

No amount of protest could cause the site on Staten Island to be cleaned up by officials in New York, nor by the federal government. Because of the toxic materials in the water, the plans to construct a power station on Staten Island had to be abandoned. Eventually, when a toxic chemicals concern across the river exploded in flames, menacing the entire population of New York City, a cleanup of the site on Staten Island was finally ordered. However, the person whose company was hired to do the cleanup was none other than a man who had been under investigation for illegal traffic in toxic wastes and for mixing toxic wastes with fuel oil, then selling it to be burned in home heating and commercial furnaces.

What occurred thereafter created an environmental tragedy, showing the serious criminal problems involved in the disposal of toxic waste. In an unlawful conspiracy, the dangerous wastes were secretly dumped into city landfills. The person whose company was hired to clean up the site was eventually convicted of bribing New York City landfill personnel.

Rain and seepage will, over time, cause the toxic elements in these landfills, built along waterways and swamplands, to leach out and eventually find their way to the ocean.

This case history is just one example of the ways in which unscrupulous persons have made and continue to make enormous profits by dumping toxic wastes directly and indirectly into the oceans. The amounts of money involved are substantial. It costs anywhere from $50 to $550 to dispose properly of a single barrel or drum containing fifty-five gallons of toxic waste. In one illegal operation, in which tank trucks containing dangerous toxic wastes were backed up on a river and their contents pumped directly into the water, each tanker held some seven thousand gallons. It required only twenty minutes to dump the wastes unlawfully into the waterway, which ran into the ocean. The criminals made a profit of fifteen thousand dollars a load for that particular kind of waste. If caught, the maximum fine they could have received (this was in the early days of toxic waste enforcement, before new and stricter laws were passed) was one thousand dollars, with no jail penalty. Even if the criminals were caught, their terrible deeds would leave them with fourteen thousand dollars in net profit.

A site described earlier—a toxic chemicals concern that exploded in flames—was involved in yet another case that had been under investigation by organized crime prosecutors. It was known as the Chemical Control case. The site was built on an industrialized delta created by the Elizabeth River on one side and the Arthur Kill on the other. The operation at Chemical Control reported itself a disposer of toxic wastes. The operators collected hazardous materials from all types of chemical, industrial, hospital, pharmaceutical, and manufacturing concerns. The site eventually became a graveyard of rusting and corroding barrels. Thousands and thousands of drums contained the most poisonous and dangerous insecticides, pesticides, and chemicals.

Organized crime decided to muscle in on this lucrative setup. The owner of Chemical Control was confronted at gunpoint and ordered out of the business. The company was taken away from him. From that moment on, until government officials executed a search warrant, additional poisonous, explosive, flammable, and other extremely dangerous wastes were hauled onto the site, until it began to overflow. The criminal operators certified the wastes were being properly disposed of, but only shipped them out again to be unlawfully dumped all over the East Coast.

Even after government officials took over the site, people acting in secret continued to bring more barrels of toxic waste onto the Chemical Control premises. Eventually, the owner

An environmental worker surveying the barrels of toxic waste along the Elizabeth River in New Jersey.

who had been forced out turned state's evidence telling how he was threatened and how illegal dumping and disposition of toxic wastes took place, thus becoming a witness for law enforcement.

It came to the chief of police's attention that certain barrels of dangerous chemicals at the site were oozing. The police chief asked the former owner for help. The barrels had been on the site when the former owner was in control, and he could identify the leaking barrels as containing dangerous and poisonous materials. It was alleged that the State of New Jersey had been told that these chemicals had been disposed of and the state had allegedly paid for their proper disposition after New Jersey officials took over the site and hired contractors to clean it up. Officials and organized crime prosecutors began closing in, checking into evidence of corruption.

Before the investigation of Chemical Control was completed, however, a fire destroyed the entire site, sending mushroom balls of flame skyward in one of the most sensational and potentially dangerous incidents in New Jersey's history. The evidence and records went up in smoke. The fire was alleged to have been set deliberately, to destroy the evidence.

Fire departments pumped millions of gallons of water on the Chemical Control fire. The chemicals and poisons were flushed into the Elizabeth River and the Arthur Kill, then carried out into the Atlantic. Health officials closed down commercial fishing over an enormous area on the East Coast, while people of the New York–New Jersey metropolitan area were stunned by the realization of the danger posed by the fire and subsequent flushing of toxic chemicals into the ocean.

Firefighters pouring millions of gallons of water onto the Chemical Control inferno. The deadly chemicals and toxic waste washed off into the Arthur Kill and Elizabeth River, contaminating the ocean.

Looking like a war-torn city, this is the site of the Chemical Control Company, or what is left of it in the aftermath of the explosion and fire.

CHARLIE Stratton, whom we met earlier, is skipper of his own boat out of Port Pleasant, New Jersey. He has been diving in the Atlantic since 1948. Charlie remembers the days when he could look down and see the bottom sand clean and shimmering eighty feet below. That's not so now. The ocean area off New York and New Jersey was a rich one for clamming, for many kinds of shellfish and fish. Yet the fishing has decreased, and, as Charlie puts it, "What they do catch, I won't eat."

One day, running out in his boat to investigate a yellow-ish substance that had been dumped offshore, Charlie found that the material was acid waste. The waste had apparently been dumped under permit, in an area known for ocean dumping of paint sludge residues and acids. It is even marked on the nautical charts as "acid waters." When Charlie returned to port and inspected his boat, he found that the screws holding the planks of his ship together had actually been eaten away by the acid.

"You don't have to do more than smell it," Charlie said, remembering an incident in 1976, when ocean dumping apparently was responsible for a complex environmental change in the ocean that caused a massive fish kill that left a hundred-and-twenty-mile-long area of the ocean dead. "It stinks and everything down there is dead.

"Anyone who doesn't believe pollution is having an effect on our lives should go to the market and have a look at the high price of fish. And many species we're told not to eat because of high mercury content or heavy metals in their flesh—that's from this ocean dumping. You can see it in the sand on the bottom. Pick up a handful; you'll see black particles deep in the sand. And there is that rotten smell—they're still dumping," Charlie said.

What Charlie Stratton knows from practical experience—from being on the ocean year after year, seeing the dramatic changes pollution has caused—scientists, environmentalists, and health officials know from their tests.

The seas and oceans of the world have been under assault since the Industrial Revolution, just before the dawn of the twentieth century. Two world wars contributed to the degradation: The spoils of chemical and bacteriological warfare, radioactive wastes, and other dangerous materials have been dumped directly into the oceans and their tributaries. Or they have been released into the atmosphere or environment in such a manner that the poisons reach the sea years, even decades, after they have been dumped.

In the last ten years, with a growing chemical industry

ever ready to supply convenience products for modern society, the by-products of manufacturing have choked the oceans. In some places the oceans have been polluted to the very limits of survival. Even sewage dumping has taken a grave toll.

In the Atlantic Ocean, in an area off Long Island called the New York Bight, the dumping of sewage sludge, the solid matter generated after the treatment of sewage wastes, has created a "Dead Sea." Nothing lives in this environment, and the sludge has been found migrating out of the dumping area close to the beautiful barrier beaches on Long Island.

Scientists are at work trying to find alternatives to ocean dumping of sewage sludge, but municipalities complain that if the sticky goo were dumped on land, the sludge collected in one year in New York City alone (about 4.5 to 5 million cubic yards) would cover an area the size of Brooklyn and Queens (almost 185 square miles) with a layer of goo two inches thick. The government has continued to put aside bans on ocean dumping while alternative methods, including land spreading, burning of sewage in furnaces, and use of sewage sludge as fertilizer are being studied.

In the Mediterranean, direct ocean dumping of raw sewage has destroyed vast reaches of the coast. The Côte d'Azur, a millionaires' playground with expensive yachts and villas overlooking the sea, is a summer tourist haven. Nonetheless, raw sewage is pumped into the water from the overpopulated tourist towns. The pollution on the French Riviera has forced the closing of many beaches. Bathers have experienced ear and eye infections, and outbreaks of skin diseases, lesions,

Every minute of every day, plumes of sewage and industrial and chemical waste pour out into the Mediterranean from the sewers of Marseille, leaving a stain that stretches for miles.

rashes, and boils have occurred. The bacterial matter in sewage waste, coupled with chemicals from industrial dumping at Marseille, has gravely imperiled the health of the Mediterranean seacoast, from France to the tip of Italy.

Professor Nardo Vicente and Philippe Tailliez, the father of modern diving and the man who introduced Jacques Cousteau to diving, are directing experiments on pollution in the Mediterranean through the environmental organization known as ECOMAIR. They have tested the waters and studied films of the effects of raw sewage dumping. At the Ile des Embiez, near Toulon in the south of France, these men and other scientists are studying the effects of oil pollution as well. Bacteria that eat oil and petroleum products may hold the key to protecting the oceans from spills and oil discharges.

While large amounts of natural oil seep into the oceans each year from deep fissures in the ocean bottom, accidents and oil spills cause a great deal more damage. Leaking tanks on land, mishaps in loading and unloading fuel, deliberate flushing of bilges and oil tanker storage cells, and collisions and accidents at sea cause great harm to the ocean environment every year. Before the price of oil skyrocketed, it was common practice for tanker captains to empty their remaining oil into the sea before going through canals, because the price of passage depended on weight. Now the oil is offloaded. Stiffer penalties have also increased the risk of unlawful dumping of oil or of flushing bilges and tanker storage cells.

Even in remote areas of the Red Sea the harmful results of oil exploration and careless loading were evident after a massive spill stained miles of virgin coastline, killing marine and bird life.

After doing its harm on the surface, oil eventually settles to the bottom of the ocean, where it destroys the spawning grounds of marine organisms and the marine plants upon

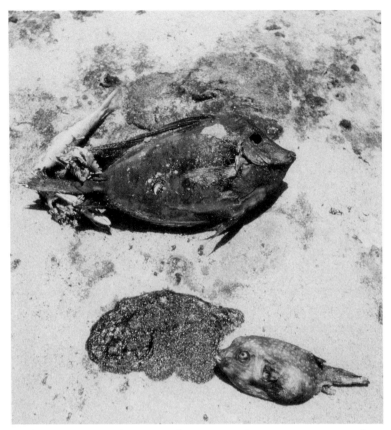

Oil spills account for great damage to the water resources of the world. Here tar-covered fish wash ashore in the Red Sea.

which they depend for food and shelter. The work of Professor Vicente on bacteria that eat oil may one day provide a solution to accidental spills that kill marine life and contaminate the seas.

The merchants of war have frequently located nuclear testing on remote islands in the Pacific. After the explosion of atomic bombs on Nagasaki and Hiroshima in 1945, some forty-three nuclear tests were conducted on Eniwetok Atoll in the Pacific as part of a continuing program to test nuclear

Charlie Stratton, here as a civilian employee of the U.S. Army, with protective gear and a metal detector, finding and removing radioactive waste in the aftermath of testing on Eniwetok Island in the Pacific. Nuclear blasts contaminate the atmosphere, causing fallout that enters the oceans and the human food chain.

weapons. To make an island available for this testing, the people of Eniwetok were taken from their homes and made to live on other islands.

The subsequent nuclear testing on Eniwetok blew vast craters in the land, sending mushroom clouds of radioactive particles into the atmosphere. Eniwetok itself became too hot radioactively for anything to exist on it. After the nuclear tests were halted there, as time passed, life began to return to the island. Fish came back slowly, and animals and plants began to appear on the destroyed reef.

The people of Eniwetok had been promised repatriation; they were told that the U.S. government would resettle them in their homeland one day. In order to keep that promise,

U.S. government officials had to comb every part of the main island and remove all radioactive objects, even those imbedded deep within the earth from the nuclear explosions. The radio-active particles were then buried in a specially constructed, protected dump site on one of the other islands. Finally, the nuclear readings were acceptable, and the people of Eniwetok were able to return to their homes.

WHAT WE have seen in this chapter are not exceptional examples of ocean damage caused by contamination with dan-gerous materials. Rather, they are typical of commonplace assaults on our ocean resources from toxic and nuclear wastes. These wastes, as we have seen, can reach the oceans directly or indirectly, the result of deliberate or accidental action.

The oceans have great powers to dilute dangerous poi-sons. After all, common sense tells us, a drop of the most deadly poison, if diluted enough, will become harmless. But the oceans in many places—even in remote areas of the world where people must depend on the sea for food—have been pushed to the very limit. They have absorbed so much harmful waste that they are contaminated, and food cannot be taken and eaten there.

Humankind must realize that ocean dumping causes con-tamination, whether it is releasing deadly materials used for warfare, dumping the by-products of our need to poison pests and insects, or even throwing away normal household materi-als, which disintegrate in time and leach out of landfills created along rivers or oceans. This activity must stop. The use of the ocean as an all-purpose dump must be halted if we are to have enough food to feed the world and survive.

Common sense tells us that when a farmer sprays crops with deadly pesticides, and it rains, the pesticides will wash off the plants and the land and enter streams and rivers, eventu-ally working their way to the sea only to poison again. But this time the pesticides will contaminate the human food chain, many miles from where the farmer has sprayed.

Perhaps a blemished orange is something we should be taught to accept. It will taste the same, and in spite of the slight imperfections caused by natural organisms, blights, rusts, or even moderate insect attacks, the fruit will be just as nutritious without a lot of dangerous spraying. Experiments with natural predators and sterile insects, irradiated in a laboratory then released into the wild population to mate with insects in the natural population with no resulting offspring, have met with great promise of success. Natural control of insects and crop diseases holds the hope for the future. For the present, however, the problem of ocean contamination from fertilizers, insecticides, and pesticides is very serious.

As Norine Rouse, the Palm Beach, Florida, diver and environmentalist, noted, "We've never seen anything like this. Every time they open up the canals and allow the run-off into the waterway, it comes out here. It is destroying the ocean reefs." What Norine and other divers saw below was appalling. Not only had the opening of Florida's inland canals, which received the run-offs from crop dusting, insecticide sprays, pesticides, and fertilizers, spread these toxins over the reefs, but silt and mud, in some places thirty-six inches thick, covered the ocean floor. The reefs that had received the major influx of sediment washed from inland canals were dead. Norine has seen the continued degradation of the marine environment in the Atlantic.

If it weren't for the northward-flowing Gulf Stream current, sweeping past Florida's coast at upward of three knots, the offshore reaches of Florida's "Gold Coast" would be polluted beyond reclamation. "It's the dumping and the run-off that's our number-one problem now," Norine said. "If we don't do something to stop it, I'm not very optimistic about the survival of these ocean reefs," she added.

People like Norine Rouse and Charlie Stratton observe the ocean every day, as do people in many parts of the world who fish for their food every day. There, catching edible fish means survival. It is everyone's responsibility to heed the warning so clearly put by Charlie Stratton, when he said, "If they don't stop this confounded dumping in the oceans, there'll be nothing left. The oceans won't be able to come back."

Criminal acts and careless and improper dumping have polluted the oceans with toxic chemicals and poisons that will never degrade. They will always remain in their poisonous state, until they are eventually consumed by humans. When that happens—when the poisons enter our food chain and enter our bodies—then we are condemned, poisoned by our own misadventure into progress.

A marine turtle off Florida's Atlantic coast burying itself in the muck that has accumulated over the reefs from the opening of inland canals. Dredging and beach erosion often account for silting over of reefs, which destroys coral and marine life.

7

Where Humans Intrude

HE opposed landfilling to construct artificial beaches a short distance from his home on Boulevard Mistral, in Toulon, France. This dumping of debris, dirt, and landfill material was even closer to his office, on the same street as the old family villa of Jules Verne. At home or at work, he was always within sight of the blue Mediterranean, a view that inspired Jules Verne to write his fantasies of things to come in *Twenty Thousand Leagues Under the Sea*. Philippe Tailliez was born in 1905, the year Jules Verne died. Only a coincidence, perhaps, but something of an omen just the same. Tailliez took up the science-fiction writer's dreams and made it possible to discover things Jules Verne only imagined.

Philippe Tailliez, the father of modern diving, was distressed. Tailliez had said, "The sea is sick, a diagnosis is required." Almost as he spoke the words, he learned of the municipality's plans to turn the rocky waterfront near his home into a park and artificial beach for tourists.

Tailliez, the first commander of the French navy's Undersea Research Group, who participated in the original bathyscaphe trials, popularized underwater filmmaking, and developed modern diving techniques and equipment, had reason to be concerned. This undersea explorer had seen the oceans of the world from the vantage point of a pioneer, before pollution, overfishing, overconstruction, and overpopulation. Now the problems that he so long sought to have corrected were being flaunted almost in front of his home and his office, the headquarters of ECOMAIR, the Mediterranean environmental body housed in the Villa Jules Verne.

All of this was very symbolic for Tailliez, a man given to symbols, who spoke of the dual ecos, of the need to balance the economy and ecology. For the eighty-one-year-old Tailliez, at an age when most people consider only their personal comfort, the current state of the marine environment presented him with the greatest challenge of his life.

Willy-nilly construction on every seashore along the Mediterranean coast, with its inherent pollution from sewage and industry, was destroying the marine plant Posidonia. This plant is considered the mother of the sea. The simple green marine grasses prevent erosion of beaches; provide food, shelter, and nesting grounds for fish; and in the shallow reaches of the tidal basins and shore areas nourished by the sun, provide oxygen through photosynthesis.

Tailliez and a team of scientists, including Jean-Marie Astier from the biology laboratory and science faculty of Saint-Jerome and Professor Nardo Vicente, Director of this laboratory (Center of Study on Marine Animal Resources) head of the Richard Oceanographic Foundation Laboratories, had conducted a study of the marine grasses.

Posidonia, a marine plant of the class Monocotyledones, produces an olivelike flower at the end of spring. The plants flourish in undisturbed water, with as many as seven thousand found in a square meter in areas called submarine meadows, pastures in the shallow coastal zones.

The scientists found that not only dikes, harbors, artificial

Philippe Tailliez, a lifelong advocate for ocean conservation, examining the Posidonia, the mother of the sea, at Port Cros, France, a marine park he created and defends as a protected reserve.

A flight over the Mediterranean coast makes it clear that marinas and over-construction have robbed important resources from the littoral, the shallow beds which nurture life and enable animals to spawn among marine Posidonia.

beaches, construction, and pollution were irreversibly destroying the sea grasses, but the grasses were also being trampled to death by the windsurfers, bathers, and pleasure boaters who descended on the coast in hordes every summer.

The small group of researchers studied and measured the sea area where Posidonia could grow. They catalogued areas that were polluted, then listed the number of ports for pleasure boats, artificial beaches, and harbor areas that were under construction. Taking the total surface area along the coastline of the French province of Var, which includes Toulon, the men found that the surface area destroyed by encroachments on the inshore, or littoral plain, was 10 percent of the area between the surface and 10 meters, and 3 percent of the area at a depth of from 10 to 20 meters. In the province of Alpes Maritimes, the province south of Toulon that includes the cities of Nice and Cannes, the researchers found 19 percent of the underwater areas destroyed between a depth of zero and 10 meters.

The researchers then determined that the artificial beaches that had been planned near Philippe Tailliez's home, in a place called Le Mourillon, would affect 236 hectares of Posidonia. In addition, they concluded that the 22 hectares of seacoast that was being landfilled for the creation of these artificial beaches would create an environmental disaster, since the fill material consisted of public garbage discharges. This would create turbidity, a zone of unclear water, over an even greater area than the actual dumping and landfilling.

The researchers also pointed out that fishermen in the area were no longer catching fish, that the commercial catch was so negligible as to make it unprofitable. They attributed this to the destruction of the undersea grasses, which are the basis of life in a healthy marine environment.

As happens too often, the advice of this small band of dedicated researchers went unheeded. Philippe Tailliez' pleas for an end to the construction of artificial beaches and pleasure ports, sewage outfalls, dumping, and building on the water's edge also fell on deaf ears. The results are evident, sad testimony to misguided progress.

Further south along the French Riviera, the city of Nice used landfill to extend the runways of its international airport, in order to accommodate jumbo jets. In order that the fill remain in position and be able to support the heavy jets, piles had to be driven into the sea. The force and amount of this pile driving was so intense that it disrupted the underwater geology of deep offshore reaches. As a result of the turmoil near shore, a deep-sea avalanche occurred far out in the Mediterranean, creating a tidal wave that flooded the construction area for the new runway. Of course, construction was resumed once the water receded. Nature's warning was more violent than the feeble voices of men dedicated to the sea, but it also went unheeded.

Memorials to humankind's great misadventures into

It is a ghost town now. "Developmental destruction," as Bonaire conservationist Robie Hensen says. Here where the environment is fragile, construction has upset the natural balance. Fill and diversion of waterways often destroys the natural controls that enable life to exist.

progress can be found everywhere. There were many to be seen on the little island of Bonaire, where marine biologist Robie Hensen drove through a ghost town of partly constructed buildings, rotting in the sun. Robie called this construction project, which was started but never finished, "Developmental Destruction."

Robie described how the land and sea merged around Kralendijk, the principal settlement town on Bonaire. The name of the town is derived from two Dutch words, meaning "coral" and "dike." Lagoons were interconnected with the sea at Kralendijk, and there had been circulation of water. For the construction project, however, the lagoons were broken up and cut off from the sea.

"This has created stagnant water," Robie explained. "As a result of, first, the construction of this road and then the building here, the stagnant water remains and mosquitos breed. There is a terrible mosquito problem in town," he said, describing how misguided development and construction on the island led to disruption of the natural system that had prevented stagnation.

On another part of the island, Robie pointed out where mangroves had been cut and pulled out to create a sand beach in front of a hotel. The hotel is rarely occupied, yet there is ample evidence of erosion where the water draining off the land carries the sand away, causing silting offshore.

These construction projects remain as testimonials to lessons to be learned from nature. We have become "sorcerers' apprentices" on a grand scale, and as we go about building here, adjusting the land and water environment there, all for supposed human convenience, we see, eventually, that very often the harm far outweighs the benefit. It is to be hoped that the people and government of Bonaire have learned this lesson well and will heed it.

FAR OFF in the Pacific, the idyllic islands of Tahiti beckon adventurers. Romantic notions remain from the days when cargo ships vied for great profits in copra and beautiful maidens lured sailors to desert their ships and live the simple life amid the splendor of tropical forests, mountains, and the sprawling Pacific Ocean. Many lagoons protect the islands from storm, also providing shallow water fishing.

As time went on, huge trees on the islands were felled

for lumber, hotel and resort complexes were built to accommodate tourists, and the tropical paradise was packaged in eight-day–seven-night tours for Everyman. With the flocks of tourists, the charm and simple beauty of the people that Paul Gauguin portrayed in his paintings, and many writers painted in words, disappeared. Only the remote islands, still isolated from the outside world, kept their customs and traditions.

Some wealthy landholders and hotelowners decided that motus, or artificial peninsulas, in front of their property would enhance the view nature had bestowed on the lagoon and also increase their land. As a result, trucks dumped dirt and debris in the lagoon on the island of Moorea, building these peninsulas out into the water. The dumping created silt and turbidity. In a very short time, the coral downstream from the artificial motus was covered with a layer of silt. Visibility in the lagoon where the dumping took place was poor. Coral polyps were choked, and the lack of clarity limited the coral's ability to grow. Soon huge stands of coral, which once formed part of the living reef and underwater beauty of the lagoon, died. With the disappearance of the reefs and coral, the fish also disappeared. What was left were unsightly and unnatural plots of land, jutting fingers into the lagoon. Brown dirt was piled up where once-pure white coral sand graced the shore. More often than not, the landholder lost interest in the motu and abandoned the project, leaving a scar on the water's edge and a wake of disruption in the underwater environment.

SUDS billowed up in great masses, looking something like clouds or cotton candy. It was laundry detergent, sudsing up at a waste-water outfall. The word "biodegradable" is bandied about today, used by those selling detergents to assure prospective purchasers that their particular suds will not cause harm to the marine environment once they are flushed away with waste water and end up at the sewage outfall. But what

Here at Brugge, Belgium, the effluent of a sewage treatment station shows the results of non-degradable soaps and detergents, a problem that causes complex changes in the marine environment that may result in fish kills and inversions.

often occurs with our soaps, washing powders, and detergents once they are discarded, even those which are said to be biodegradable, is reason for concern.

Many laundry detergents and soaps contain phosphates and sulfonates, chemicals that are nutrients for plants. These phosphates and sulfonates do not degrade when waste water is processed in sewage treatment plants and then pumped out into streams and rivers, seas and oceans. Marine algae, which thrive on these chemical wastes, bloom in great numbers in direct proportion to the increased food that comes their way. As a result, there are so many algae that an imbalance occurs in the marine environment, and the algae deprive higher forms of life of oxygen. This can result in massive fish and invertebrate kills. The process is called eutrophication.

Marine algae produce oxygen during daylight hours by photosynthesis, but at night they consume oxygen. Bacteria feeding on dead and decomposing algae also bloom in great numbers, and in the biological process in which the bacteria eat the algae, they also consume oxygen. This imbalance in the marine environment is caused by the introduction of nutrients through nondegradable soaps and detergents. These disruptions destroy sea life.

WE often discard things without a thought given to the way our seashore, marshlands, oceans, bays, lagoons, or harbors will look, or what consequences the discards will have on the marine environment. Discarded plastic bags have been swallowed by marine animals and have choked and killed turtles and cetaceans. Nets abandoned, lost, or cut free by fishermen have trapped whales or have killed fish that get tangled in them as they drift for years in the sea or become hung up on shipwrecks or obstructions below.

Old cars, refrigerators, and other junk that is no longer

wanted is often discarded along the waterfront, simply pushed into the ocean. We have made a mess of our most valuable resource on this planet, a mess that could have been avoided simply by giving some thought to the consequences of our actions.

As we've discussed, even the proper disposal of garbage, eventually collected and landfilled in dumps built on marsh-lands and along bays and harbors, continues to pollute the oceans for many, many years, even after a landfill is abandoned. The seepage of dangerous elements from garbage continues to release millions of gallons of leachate concentrated with heavy metals and other dangerous elements into the water.

More people means more trash, and more nondegradable trash, such as plastics and batteries, items that are a result of our high-tech lifestyles. No matter how we view the problem, trash is trouble, and discards in or near the marine environment not only pollute and degrade our water resources but also decrease their beauty, a source of inspiration and pleasure for all of us.

DEFORESTATION—cutting trees and removing plants and bushes, even in mountains many miles from the oceans—has also affected the marine environment. In areas near the sea-shore, roads have been built along the ocean, and huge con-crete condominiums, hotels, and apartment complexes loom up where once there was only a tangle of sprawling sea oats, grass, mangroves, or bushes.

Junk. It doesn't look nice and it isn't good for the environment. Even our memorials to progress are offset by discards from our wasteful lifestyles. This is the Brooklyn Bridge in New York Harbor.

As a result of deforestation, extensive beach erosion and run-offs from the land have occurred. Rain is no longer retained by the root systems of the plants that used to grow along the oceanfront, and the plants are no longer there to protect the land from the forces of sea and wind. In some areas, even the slightest storm does great damage, since the natural barriers that have kept the waters retained and the oceans in check have been uprooted in the name of progress.

So much damage has been done to so many beaches by visitors that certain areas have been posted, and sand dunes have been placed off-limits to hikers and trail-bike riders. Continual invasions by people destroy the dune barriers that required centuries to accumulate. Warning signs are also prominently displayed, telling people not to disturb or pick the sea oats or marine grasses growing in the sand, which serve to hold the beaches and prevent erosion.

The oceans are to be enjoyed by visitors, not invaded by hordes of bikers with noisy motorcycles gouging out natu-

We have depleted the world's forests. Here trees felled on the island of Tahiti required centuries to grow. Deforestation has a telling and dramatic effect on run-off and soil erosion, directly affecting the oceans.

On the island of Martinique in the French West Indies the daily output from the manufacture of construction material stains and spoils the beautiful Caribbean coastline.

ral barriers that protect the seashore and offer shelter to marine birds and other creatures, including nesting marine turtles.

In only the last twenty-five years, 50 percent of the world's forests have been harvested or destroyed by human activities. Where hardwoods were once plentiful in tropical countries, whole forests are being cut down and tropical jungles denuded of trees. What is left are scars on the land. These areas of forest served as a watershed, providing undeveloped tropical countries with water retention. Massive muddy run-offs, careening down the deforested mountains into streams and rivers to the ocean, pollute it with land soil, disturbing the balance in the sea, while the fertile soil from the land is washed away. These new nutrients in the tropical seas change the balance of nature and create environmental problems, just as detergents cause eutrophication. Deforestation has destroyed traditional fishing, while depleting the land of valuable nutrients and fertile soil.

A VERY complex effect on the oceans of the world is being caused by pollution of the atmosphere with vaporized gases. This results from the burning of fossil fuels in cars, airplanes, industrial furnaces, and the like, as well as vaporized chemical wastes. The phenomenon is called "the greenhouse effect."

Dr. F. G. Walton Smith, president of the International Oceanographic Foundation and former dean of the University of Miami School of Oceanographic and Atmospheric Science, put it clearly when he wrote, "Two closely related problems facing the human race today in which the ocean is involved are the approaching end of our supplies of fossil fuels and the harmful additions of carbon dioxide to the atmosphere brought about by their combustion, the so-called greenhouse effect."

Dr. Smith points out the potential for calamity unless alternative fuel sources are found from the sun or from safe nuclear power, stating that " . . . the ocean is the only continuously operating reservoir of solar energy."

The greenhouse effect is gradually causing the Earth to heat up. The sun's rays strike the Earth, and they are reflected off, back into the atmosphere. Gases in the atmosphere deflect the rays back again to earth, almost in the same way a mirror reflects light. The re-reflected rays strike the Earth again and cause increased heating. It is the same process that takes place inside a greenhouse.

Scientists feel that this heating will eventually cause the

ice in the polar regions to melt. The oceans will then rise all over the world, creating flooding and submerging vast areas.

Dr. Smith says, "The greenhouse effect is a highly complicated phenomenon involving both ocean and atmosphere. At present, the probable extent of atmospheric heating and the rate at which the heating effect may bring about world disasters are impossible to determine, without further research. This only makes a solution more urgent," he concludes.

Charlie Stratton, whom we met earlier, an engineer with the U.S. government and a man who has been diving the Atlantic waters off the New Jersey coast for many years, attended a conference held by the New Jersey Marine Sciences Consortium, on the effects of the sea-level rise expected as a result of the greenhouse effect. "Their evidence was ample in convincing us that a substantial portion of our state will be given up to the sea. Included in these losses will be Atlantic City, the Meadowlands Sports Complex, our beaches and barrier islands, which are already eroding, major sea ports, and much, much more," Charlie reported.

The threat is very real. As carbon dioxide increases in the atmosphere, and as other gases, such as sulfur dioxide, methane, and nitrous oxide also increase, the greenhouse effect intensifies.

"Two of the most significant mechanisms for processing carbon dioxide are ocean phytoplankton [plants] and coral reef builders. It is estimated that approximately 80 percent of the removal of carbon dioxide from the environment takes place in the shallow waters of a healthy ocean, from the beach to a depth of three hundred feet," Charlie explains. "It is here that sunlight provides the energy for sea life to process carbon dioxide, removing it from the atmosphere. It is also here, in the shallow coastal waters, that man has decided to transfer his unwanted wastes and filth by continued and increased dumping of human wastes, industrial wastes, acids, dredge spoils, oxides, and industrial cleaners, turning this bountiful ecosystem into an unbelievable, inhospitable sump," Charlie stated emphatically.

His conclusion is inevitable. "In so doing, we have very effectively blocked the sunlight from penetrating, thereby eliminating the phytoplankton and corals that were doing the converting," Charlie said.

Whether scientists would completely agree with Charlie's plain talk about the complex causes and potential solutions to the greenhouse effect is not as important as the realization that the problem of a buildup of carbon dioxide in the earth's atmosphere is very serious. The sun's rays are being trapped and bounced back between this atmospheric layer and the earth. As a result, the snowcaps and frozen polar ice masses may eventually melt. A long-term solution is required, and responsible action must be taken quickly to avert this calamity, which respected scientists like Dr. Smith see as the inevitable result of burning fossil fuels.

THERE IS an island in the far reaches of the Pacific, located between Guam and the Philippines, where civilization came on the heels of World War II, changing an ancient culture, economy, and ocean environment. The situation there describes the problems and issues of our times.

It is the land of stone money, where even today debts of honor and land transfers take place with the exchange of huge chunks of stone, round and with a hole in the middle, quarried 250 miles to the east, on the island of Palau. In olden days, men from the island of Yap would sail across the open ocean to Palau in their frail sailing canoes, to quarry the stone and bring it back to their island, where it was revered for its scarcity and the danger and risk the men took in obtaining it. Today Yap's stone money is largely symbolic; the grass

The island of Yap has become a tin can junkyard and a tin can economy.

skirts worn by the women are slowly passing out of vogue, as generations of young Yapese watch a form of cable television and drink soda out of aluminum cans.

Sewage waste clogs the waterways of the principal settlement on Yap. Silt from dredging and bulldozing for a new and larger dock covers the island's reefs in the lagoon near the site of the construction, and a great scar cuts across the middle of the island, where a tropical forest is being uprooted and bulldozed for a longer airstrip to accommodate military jets. All this is happening on an island with only thrice weekly eastbound air passenger service and two small hotels, unable to handle more than a handful of visitors at a time.

Yap has become a tin-can junkyard, with piles of aluminum cans in varying stages of decomposition littering the waterfront along with junked cars and trash, discards from an import economy that the elected governor of Yap says must stop.

"We are trying to get away from Coke. In our store we have fresh coconuts. I hope we will get away from Coke and drink our natural drink, which is better for your body," Governor John deAvila Mangefel says. "We get roughly six million dollars a year for this state from the United States. We turn around and give most of that back in exchange for rice, Coca-Cola, beer, cigarettes, and construction material. What we are trying to do is use that money for development. To develop ourselves. . . . More than a million dollars is spent each year for fuel to run the power plant. We are looking into windmills and alternative means of getting power," the governor says, and means it.

Yap is still part of the Federated States of Micronesia, a successor to the Trust Territory status that occurred after World War II, with the United States overseeing Yap and other islands in Micronesia under a United Nations mandate.

"The most valuable thing in our culture," Governor Mangefel stresses, "is our relationship with each other. Whether you are living in a concrete house with electricity is not important. It is the way we treat each other. People in the villages help each other when a person gets sick. I've heard that in New York if somebody falls down, nobody will help. In Yap we try to preserve human kindness. When you go into a village, the first thing they ask you is if you have a coconut to drink. Next, do you have betel nut to chew. This is a very rich thing," the governor explains.

"We are going to stop that dredging business," the governor declares emphatically. "Once we get the road and the airport and the dock finished, we have to get that dredging

Governor Mangefel hopes to reverse the trend.

stopped. The dock will probably be all we'll ever need for perhaps the next hundred years. Once the dock is finished a ship will call once a month or once every two months," he adds, dismayed that the construction projects and progress in general are causing environmental damage to the island and its culture.

Yap is a place of contrasts. It is a place where progress has spoiled the remnants of a very rich heritage and culture, just as it has damaged the once pristine environment. It is the island where the sole survivor of a wrecked ship drifted ashore in 1878, and was nursed back to health by the people. When the shipwrecked sailor, David Dean O'Keefe, regained his strength, he saw that there was a fortune to be made on Yap in the copra trade. Yap also had vast stocks of coconuts, and the waters around the island abounded with sea cucumbers, a delicacy in the Orient. The only problem was that no one had yet succeeded in getting the people on the island to want to work.

The only thing of importance to the people on Yap was their once-yearly trip across the ocean to Palau, to quarry their precious stone money. When he was fully recovered, O'Keefe embarked on a passing steamer and went to Hong Kong, where he found a partner who equipped him with a sailing bark. With the vessel he sailed back to Yap. He offered to take the men of the island to Palau, where they could quarry the stone and bring it back in large quantities to the island in the safety of the large sailing ship.

The people of Yap were overjoyed at this prospect and set out at once for Palau. When great quantities of stone money had been unloaded on Yap, David Dean O'Keefe was proclaimed King. His Majesty O'Keefe promptly put the islanders to work for him, gathering coconuts and drying them and preparing the copra, which he took in his ship to the Orient and sold at great profit. When the Germans occupied Yap at the outbreak of World War I, His Majesty O'Keefe disappeared. Some thought he had left in his sailing ship, but O'Keefe was never seen or heard from again. What he left behind was stone money quarried and brought back to Yap the easy way.

Today on Yap, the people know which stone money was collected in the traditional way—by men of the village risking their lives in frail sailing canoes in the perils of the sea. They also know which stone money came to them without great effort—the money brought back in O'Keefe's ship has much

Traditional values symbolized by Yap's famous stone money and a traditional lifestyle depend on clean and healthy ocean resources.

less value even today. There is a parallel lesson in the values now being placed on imported culture and progress, which has robbed the Yapese of their own values and at the same time polluted their island and water environment.

"This is an upside down economy. It is a false economy," Governor Mangefel says. "We don't produce the money. We get the money from the United States, then give it back to get rice and Coca-Cola. We are trying to stop that. We don't know how. We are trying to change. Our air and water is still clean, but it is starting to get polluted. Our most valuable thing is our culture and custom," the governor stresses, folding a betel nut into a leaf and powdering it with lime. He pauses, examines the wad, then inserts it between his gum- and or-ange-stained lips and teeth.

We have intruded on tradition. We have intruded on the environment, which has upset the balance of nature in the oceans and in cultures that depend on the sea. When we intrude, we must be sure that the progress we bring is more valuable than the culture we destroy. As in all things, since we never really can be sure what will occur in the long run, we must intrude carefully, so as not to destroy anything before we understand the importance of life around and under the sea.

8

Things We Can Do

Hy·dro·struc·ture   (Hi'drō, hi'drs, + struk' chēr) [<Gr.
Hydōr, water + L. structura < structus, PP. of struere, to
heap together, arrange; cf. strew], 1. manner of building,
constructing or organizing in water, 2. something built or
constructed in the seas or oceans as in the construction of
artificial reefs, 3. any manner of manmade submarine
habitat constructed to furnish shelter and attachable
surfaces for marine organisms, 4. the fabrication of an
artificial underwater sanctuary for the promulgation,
preservation, conservation or harvest of food from the sea,
—SYN. see MARICULTURE , CONSERVATION.

HYDROSTRUCTURE is
only a word, yet it represents the commitment we must adopt
toward building in the sea for a better tomorrow. Other words
have come into the conservationist's vocabulary, such as aqua-
culture and mariculture. These words denote farming in the
sea, raising aquatic plants and animals to supply food for
the world.

Whatever it is called, developing ocean resources—ex-
panding the oceans' ability to support and sustain life—is
the future. Protecting these marine resources will mean the
difference between life and death for millions of people. We
are at the crossroads, at the turning point. If, as you read

these words, there is a commitment and determination by nations and the people of those nations to conserve and protect our present ocean resources and to develop conservation projects, then immediate and future needs for food can be met. If, as you read these words, nothing has been done and the world attitude continues on its greedy, self-interested path, then all humankind will suffer.

Look at pictures of little children suffering from starvation, and you will know that we all hurt through their suffering. Diseases such as Kwashiorkor, where the frail body swells and the skin peels off, is caused by lack of protein. Marasmus, where the child's body wastes away, is caused by debilitating malnutrition.

The spirit within us is diminished by the pain of starving children. It is our pain as well. There is no choice but to ask: What can I do—the problems are so complex and human nature so difficult to change?

Subscribe to The Ocean Charter. Become a free citizen of the seas. Pledge yourself to the protection of our oceans in peril. Be responsible first for yourself and your actions. Make this simple pledge, then join with others to undertake constructive projects that will enable the oceans to survive.

THE CONCEPT of putting structures on the ocean bottom to create artificial reefs is not new. Anyone snorkling over a shipwreck that has been underwater for any length of time notices the abundance of life attached to the hull and the myriad of fish swimming around the wreck. Knowing fishermen cast their nets perilously close to shipwrecks and underwater obstructions. In the sea, having a home means survival. Fish congregate around underwater obstructions of any kind, whether rocky islands in the undersea, shipwrecks, or concrete structures that have been deliberately placed on the bottom to serve as artificial reefs.

A marine community begins with invertebrate life. Plant and animal life attach and grow on a substrate or fixed base. These organisms are the food for larger species. They provide the living community that creates a healthy, well-balanced underwater environment.

As Frederic Dumas explained, the area where fish life abounds in the sea is relatively narrow. The shallow, inshore areas, where sunlight penetrates and marine plants can grow, is the ocean's most productive garden. Organisms can attach to rocks or other structures, usually in areas near the shore. The largest areas of the ocean are nonproductive for life in the sea; they are too deep, or with a bottom composed of sand. These areas will not sustain a complex marine community.

In the vast deep oceans, there are surface dwellers, of course, plankton upon which larger animals feed. Krill-rich waters are home to great whales. But for practical use of the seas as farms, it is the shallow reaches that are most important. Areas near shore or that extend out like plateaus, slowly sloping down like the Continental Shelf of the Atlantic, provide shallow ocean water where life can develop.

Here in the offshore reaches of the oceans where the water is relatively shallow, perhaps seventy to two hundred feet deep, artificial reef projects have been successful. Fish havens have been created where life is attracted to an undersea oasis affording food and shelter. It is a question of using the ocean space productively.

Old shipwrecks have been deliberately sunk to serve as artificial reefs. These structures are fine, but they are not permanent. Concrete construction rubble has also been used with great success in building artificial reefs in the sea. Junk like old rubber tires, even wrecked car bodies cleaned of debris and oil, have been used to create artificial reefs. The tires, however, have often broken apart in a short time, and the

Building in the sea for a better tomorrow is what hydrostructure is all about. Here in a deliberately scuttled shipwreck, marine life attaches and grows, attracting larger organisms and fish that feed on them and seek shelter amid the wreckage.

old car bodies deteriorated, making them undesirable as reef-building materials.

Large concrete pylons that look something like giant jacks have been specially fabricated for sinking as artificial reefs off the coast of Australia. These reef-building programs have met with a great deal of success.

In addition to building hydrostructures in the sea to support life, farming the sea has proved successful in many parts of the world. One of the oldest sea-farming projects is the cultured pearl industry. Oysters are seeded with a grain of sand or a bead and then placed on stringers, to be harvested when the pearl develops. Trout hatcheries raise fingerlings, releasing them every summer prior to the start of fishing season. Other projects, such as salmon raising in places like Scotland, have also met with a great deal of success. We must continue to experiment with new ways to farm the sea and increase our efforts to protect the oceans' natural resources.

IN 1609, when Henry Hudson sailed into what would become New York Harbor, he wrote in his journal of the crystal-clear sparkling waters of the river that would eventually bear his name. Now polluted with polychlorinated biphenyls (PCBs) and other toxic elements, such as heavy metals, the Hudson has strict bans against taking and selling fish. Warn-

We will come to farm the sea for food; already promising experiments have been conducted and many sea farming projects around the world successfully raise oysters, fish, and other shellfish.

ings have been posted by health authorities cautioning against eating certain game fish from the ocean more than once a week. Authorities warn of the risk of accumulation in human tissues of poisons that the fish have absorbed in their flesh and tissues, the result of eating contaminated food.

Surfacing from a dive twenty miles out into the Atlantic where the water was only eighty feet deep because of the Continental Shelf, Charlie Stratton was dismayed. Pollution had created an imbalance called an inversion, which had smothered life in this part of the ocean for hundreds of square miles. It resulted in a massive fish and marine life kill.

"Everything is dead," Charlie said, holding up a huge dead lobster and other marine animals he had recovered from the bottom. He would ice the dead animals and bring them to a marine lab for diagnosis of the problem.

"I've never seen anything this bad. I won't eat seafood anymore. I've been getting sick, and I couldn't say why until now," Charlie declared, looking down at the dead and putrefying lobster. "We've hit the bottom of the barrel," Charlie sighed. "I've been diving here since 1948, and this is the absolute worst I've ever seen."

Saying that the oceans are polluted is not enough. As responsible citizens of this Planet Ocean, we must join together to become the vanguard of the oceans, sentinels of the seas. We must pledge ourselves to The Ocean Charter, then learn, join, and undertake conservation projects with responsible organizations to help turn the tide—to protect our most valuable resource, the last wilderness on earth.

For anyone who has had the pleasure of discovering the beauty of a tropical reef, the sea's harmony and balance offers a lesson. We must pledge ourselves as guardians of this underwater wilderness, sentinels of our last frontier.

BIBLIOGRAPHY

A bibliography is a jumping-off place for further study. Since current issues involving the oceans and environment are frequently treated in the daily press, a good place to start is at your local library. The reference librarian there can show you where to find newspaper and periodical indexes. The *New York Times,* for example, is indexed and available on microfilm. Your librarian can show you how to use the index and microfilm readers to find articles in back issues. A look through the magazine racks in libraries or bookstores will also suggest current periodicals that feature articles on ocean topics.

Organization Periodicals

Many organizations publish magazines and offer special services for members as part of a modest annual membership fee. A few organizations whose goals include ocean conservation are:

INTERNATIONAL OCEANOGRAPHIC FOUNDA-TION, 3979 Rickenbacker Causeway, Virginia Key, Miami, FL 33149. As part of the University of Miami, IOF will help answer questions about career possibilities in oceanography and marine science. They operate Planet Ocean in Miami, an oceanography museum and exhibit center. Their publications include *Sea Frontiers* and *Sea Secrets,* informative and beautifully presented magazines about the seas and oceans. The editors of *Sea Secrets* will answer questions about ocean animals and events.

OCEANIC SOCIETY, 2001 West Main Street, Stamford, CT 06902. The Oceanic Society participates in many environmental programs, such as the Long Island (New York–Connecticut) Sound Task Force. Their magazine, *Oceans,* brings ocean topics to the reader in beautiful color, with informative articles and photographs.

COUSTEAU SOCIETY, 930 West 21st Street, Norfolk, VA 23517. The Society focuses on ocean environmental issues and problems. Their magazines, *Calypso Log* and *Dolphin Log* (for young readers) provides up-to-date information on Society expeditions and ocean problems.

Books

While your local librarian will be able to suggest many other books to supplement your reading, here is a list of some that will be of interest for further study:

Block, Alan A. and Frank R. Scarpitti. *Poisoning for Profit: The Mafia and Toxic Waste in America.* New York: William Morrow & Co., 1985.

Borgese, Elizabeth Mann. *The Drama of the Oceans.* New York: Harry N. Abrams, 1975.

——— *Sea Farm.* New York: Harry N. Abrams, 1980.

Cousteau, Jacques-Yves, and Philippe Diole. *The Whale.* New York: Doubleday, 1972.

Epstein, Samuel, Lester O. Brown, and Carl Pope. *Hazardous Waste in America.* San Francisco: Sierra Club Books, 1982.

Fine, John Christopher. *Exploring the Sea.* Medford, N.J.: Plexus Publishing, Inc., 1982.

Herman, Louis M. *Cetacean Behavior.* New York: John Wiley & Sons, 1980.

Kiefer, Irene. *Poisoned Land.* New York: Atheneum, 1985.

Line, Les, and George Reiger. *The Audubon Society Book of Marine Wildlife.* New York: Harry N. Abrams, 1980.

Poynter, Margaret, and Donald Collins. *Under the High Seas.* New York: Atheneum, 1983.

Roessler, Carl. *Coral Kingdoms.* New York: Harry N. Abrams, 1986.

Some Universities and Graduate Schools Offering Specialties in Ocean Science

A booklet entitled "Training and Careers in Marine Science" with additional listings may be obtained by writing the International Oceanographic Foundation at the address on page 134.

University of Miami, Rosenstiel School of Marine and Atmospheric Science, 4600 Rickenbacker Causeway, Miami, Florida 33149.

Woods Hole Oceanographic Institution, Woods Hole, Massachusetts 02543.

Columbia University (Lamont-Doherty Geological Laboratory, located in Palisades, New York), 435 West 116th Street, New York, New York 10027.

Scripps Institution (University of California System), La Jolla, California 92037.

University of Rhode Island, Kingston, Rhode Island 02881.

University of Hawaii, Honolulu, Hawaii 96822.

University of North Carolina, Chapel Hill, North Carolina 27514.

INDEX

11662